New York Times, #1 Amazon, *USA Today*, and *Publishers Weekly* bestselling author Freida McFadden is a practicing physician specializing in brain injury. Freida's work has been selected as one of Amazon Editor's Best Books of the Year, and she has been a Goodreads Choice Award nominee. Her novels have been translated into more than thirty languages. Freida lives with her family and black cat in a centuries-old three-story home overlooking the ocean.

ALSO BY FREIDA MCFADDEN

Ward D
The Inmate
The Housemaid
The Housemaid's Secret
Do You Remember?
Do Not Disturb
The Locked Door
Want to Know a Secret?
One by One
The Wife Upstairs
The Perfect Son
The Ex
The Surrogate Mother
Brain Damage
Baby City
Suicide Med
The Devil Wears Scrubs
The Devil You Know

NEVER LIE

FREIDA McFADDEN

PENGUIN BOOKS
An imprint of Penguin Random House

PENGUIN BOOKS

USA | Canada | UK | Ireland | Australia
New Zealand | India | South Africa | China | Singapore

Penguin Books is part of the Penguin Random House group of companies whose addresses can be found at global.penguinrandomhouse.com

Published by Penguin Random House India Pvt. Ltd
4th Floor, Capital Tower 1, MG Road,
Gurugram 122 002, Haryana, India

Penguin
Random House
India

This edition published in 2024 by Penguin Random House India

10 9 8 7 6 5 4 3 2

The views and opinions expressed in this book are the author's own and the facts are as reported by him/her which have been verified to the extent possible, and the publishers are not in any way liable for the same.

ISBN 9780143464525

Typeset by Digiultrabooks Pvt. Ltd.
Printed at Gopsons Papers Pvt. Ltd., Noida

www.penguin.co.in

FSC www.fsc.org MIX Paper from responsible sources FSC® C191020

To my family

PROLOGUE

ADRIENNE

Everybody lies.

Years ago, a psychological experiment was devised to estimate the prevalence of untruthful behaviour. It involved a broken vending machine.

Subjects were informed that the vending machine was malfunctioning. If they put in a dollar, the faulty machine would dispense candy but then return their dollar. Subjects who used the vending machine found this to be absolutely true. They dispensed one, two, three, or even four pieces of free candy and then retrieved their money from the machine.

There was a sign on the vending machine. The sign read 'To report any malfunctions with this machine, please call this number.' Unbeknownst to the subjects, the number provided belonged to one researcher in the study.

Take a guess how many of the subjects called this number to report the broken machine.

Zero.

That's right. Not even one of the dozens of subjects was honest enough to call the number and report the broken vending machine. Each one of them took their free candy and moved on.

As I said, everybody lies.

There are many easily identified signs that a person is lying, especially if they are an unskilled liar. As a trained psychiatrist, I am intimately familiar with these signs. It's almost too easy to spot them:

Liars fidget.

The tone of their voice or speech patterns changes.

Liars offer too much information, babbling on with excessive detail to convince themselves or others of what they are saying.

Machines have been built to recognize these patterns and identify them. However, even the best lie detector has a 25 per cent rate of error. I am far more accurate than that. If you listen to the audiotapes of my patient encounters, you can't always tell. On tape, you miss the important visual cues. Avoiding eye contact, for example, or covering their mouth or eyes. But if you are my patient, and you are sitting in my office talking to me, I can watch your face and your gestures and listen to the pitch of your voice.

I will know the truth. I always know. Never lie to me.

CHAPTER 1

TRICIA

PRESENT DAY

We're hopelessly lost and my husband won't admit it.

I can't say this is atypical behaviour for Ethan. We've been married for six months—still newlyweds—and 90 per cent of the time, he's the perfect husband. He knows all the most romantic restaurants in town, he still surprises me with flowers, and when he asks me about my day, he actually listens to my answer and asks appropriate follow-up questions.

But the other 10 per cent of the time, he is so stubborn I could scream.

'You missed the turn for Cedar Lane,' I tell him. 'We passed it, like, half a mile down the road.'

'*No*.' A scary-looking vein bulges in Ethan's neck. 'It's up ahead. We didn't pass it.'

I let out a frustrated huff as I clutch the printed directions to the house in Westchester, courtesy of our real estate agent, Judy. Yes, we do have GPS, but that signal went out about ten minutes ago. Now all we've got to rely on are these written directions. It's like living in the Stone Age.

Well, Ethan wanted something out of the way. He's getting his wish.

The worst part is that it's *snowing*. It started a few hours ago, back when we were leaving Manhattan. When we left, they were cute little white flakes that evaporated on contact with the ground. Over the last hour, the flakes have quadrupled in size. They're not cute any more.

Now that we have turned off the highway, this more deserted, narrow road is slick with snow. And it's not like Ethan drives a truck. His BMW has gorgeous hand-stitched leather seats but only front-wheel drive, and he's not incredibly skilled at driving in the snow either. If we skidded, he probably wouldn't even know whether to turn *into* the skid or *out* of the skid. (Into the skid, right?)

As if on cue, the BMW skids on a patch of slushy ice.

Ethan's fingers are bloodless on the steering wheel. He rights the vehicle, but my heart is pounding. The snow is getting really bad. He pulls over to the side of the road and holds out his hand to me.

'Let me see those directions.'

Dutifully, I hand over the slightly crumpled piece of paper. I wish he had let me drive. Ethan would never admit I'm better at navigating than he is. 'I think we passed the turn, Ethan.'

He looks down at a sheet of typed directions. Then he squints out the windshield. Even with the wipers going full speed and our high beams on, the visibility is horrible.

Now that the sun has dropped in the sky, we can only see about ten feet ahead of us. Everything past that is pure white. 'No. I see how to get there.'

'Are you sure?'

Instead of answering my question, he grumbles, 'You should have checked the weather before we got on the road.'

'Maybe we should turn back?' I press my hands between my knees. 'We can view the house another time.' Like when there isn't a freaking blizzard raging outside the car.

My husband whips his head around and glares at me like I have lost my mind. 'Tricia, we've been driving for almost *two hours* to get here. We're about ten minutes away, and now you want to *turn around and go home*?'

That's another thing I have learned about Ethan in the six months we've been married. Once he gets an idea in his head to do something, he does not back down until it's done. I suppose I could see it as a good thing. I wouldn't want to be married to a man who left a bunch of half-finished projects around the house.

I'm still learning about Ethan. All my girlfriends scolded me for marrying him too quickly. We met in a coffee shop one day—I tripped and spilled my drink right next to his table, and he insisted on buying me a new one. It was one of those love-at-first-sight deals. When I saw him, I fell hard for his blonde hair streaked with even blonder strands. His blue eyes were the colour of the sky on a clear day and rimmed with pale lashes. And his strong Roman nose kept him from being too pretty. When he smiled at me, I was a goner. We spent the next six hours together, sharing coffee, then later that same evening, he took me out to dinner. That night, I broke up with my boyfriend of over a year, explaining apologetically that I had met the man I was going to marry.

Nine months later, my coffee shop Romeo and I were married. Six months later, we're moving out to the sub-urbs. Our entire relationship has been on fast forward.

But so far, no regrets. The more I learn about Ethan, the more I fall in love with him. And he feels the same way about me. It's so amazing sharing my life with him.

Except for the one big secret he doesn't know about yet.

'Fine,' I say. 'Let's find the house.'

Ethan hands me the sheet of directions. He throws the BMW back into drive. 'I know exactly where to go. It's right up ahead.'

That remains to be seen.

He drives slower this time, both to account for the snow and to keep from missing the turn, which I'm certain that he already missed about half a mile down the road. I keep my eyes on the road as well, even though the windshield is now caked with snow. I try to think warm, dry thoughts.

'There!' Ethan cries. 'I see it!'

I lean forward in my seat, straining the seat belt. He *sees* it? Sees *what*, exactly? Is he wearing invisible snow/night-vision goggles? Because all I can see is snow, and then beyond that, more snow, and beyond *that*, blackness. But then he slows down, and sure enough, there's a little path leading into a wooded area, and the high beams illuminate a sign that's almost obscured by snow. I can just barely make out the words as he takes the turn just a bit too fast.

Cedar Lane.

What do you know—Ethan was right all along. I was sure he had passed the turn for Cedar, but he hadn't. It's right here. Although now that we're on the tiny narrow road to get to the house, I am concerned the BMW won't make it. When I look over at my husband's face, I can tell he is worried about the same thing. The path to the house is barely paved, and now it's thick with snow.

'We should tell Judy to keep the showing quick,' I say. 'We don't want to get stuck here.'

Ethan bobs his head in agreement. 'I have to be honest. I wanted something out of the way, but this is insane. I mean, it's like we're in the middle of ...'

His voice trails off midsentence. I can only imagine he was going to point out that we are in the middle of nowhere. But before he can get out the words, his mouth falls open. Because the house has finally come into view.

And it's unbelievable.

The listing on Judy's website mentioned that it's two stories tall, plus an attic, but that description doesn't do justice to this sprawling estate. The ceilings must be extremely high, because the steep gable roof seems to scrape against the sky, heavy with snow. The sides of the house are lined with pointed-arch windows that give it a look of a cathedral rather than a place where people live. Ethan's jaw looks like it might unhinge.

'Jesus,' he breathes. 'Can you imagine *living* in a place like that?'

I may have known my husband for only just over a year, but I recognize the look on his face. He's not asking a rhetorical question. He *wants* to live in this house. We have dragged poor Judy across half of Westchester and Long Island because no place we have seen has quite lived up to the picture Ethan has in his head. But now …

'You like it?' I ask.

'Don't you think it's great? I mean, look at the place.' I open my mouth to agree with him. This house is undeniably beautiful. It's huge and elegant and remote—all the things we have been searching for. It's a perfect home to fill up with children, which is our eventual goal. I want to tell Ethan that I love the house as much as he does. That when Judy arrives, we should make her an offer on the spot.

But I can't do that.

Because as I stare out at this sprawling estate, a sick feeling comes over me. So sick that I cover my mouth and take a deep breath to keep from losing my lunch all over the BMW's expensive upholstery. I have never felt this way before. Not about any of the dozens of empty houses we have toured over the last couple of months. I have never had a feeling this strong.

Something terrible has happened in this house.

'Oh crap,' Ethan says.

I take another shaky breath, pushing away another wave of nausea. That's when I notice we have stopped moving. The front wheels spin determinedly, but it's no use. The car is stuck.

'The roads are too slippery,' he says. 'We can't get any traction.'

I hug myself and shiver, even though the heat is blasting. 'What should we do?

'Well …' He reaches out to wipe some condensation off the windshield. 'We're pretty close to the house. We can walk it.'

Easy for him to say. He's not wearing Manolo Blahnik boots.

'Also, it looks like Judy is already here,' he adds. 'Really? I don't see her car.'

'Yeah, but the lights are on. She must be parked in the garage.'

I squint through the fogged windshield at the house. Now that I'm looking closer, I can see a single light glowing in one of the upstairs windows. That's odd. If a real estate agent were showing a house, wouldn't she turn the lights on *downstairs*? But the entire first floor of the house is dark. There's only that one light upstairs.

Once again, I shiver.

'Come on,' Ethan says. 'We're better off inside. It's not like we can spend the night in the car. We'll run out of gas and freeze to death.'

Not an appealing thought. I'm starting to regret this entire trip. What was I thinking coming out here? But Ethan loves the house. Maybe this will all work out.

'Fine,' I say. 'Let's walk.'

CHAPTER 2

Oh my God, it's so cold.

As soon as I open the passenger-side door to the BMW, I deeply regret agreeing to walk to the house. I'm wearing my Ralph Lauren wool-coat that goes down to my knees, but I may as well be wearing a sheet of paper because the wind seems to go right through me, even when I pull up my hood.

But the worst part is my feet. I am wearing leather boots, but they're not really *snow* boots, if you know what I mean. They add a much-appreciated three inches to my height, and they look gorgeous with skinny blue jeans, but they do absolutely nothing to protect my feet from the foot of snow now surrounding them.

Why oh why did I buy a pair of stylish boots that have no ability to actually function as boots? I'm starting to deeply regret all my life choices at the moment. My mother always said not to leave the house in shoes you can't walk a mile in.

'You okay, Tricia?' Ethan asks. 'You're not cold, are you?'

He crinkles his forehead, perplexed by my chattering teeth and lips that are slowly turning blue. He's wearing the black ski jacket he bought last month, and although I can't see his feet, I'm fairly sure *his* boots are big and warm. I want to wring his neck for making me do this, but that would involve taking my hands out of my deep pockets and would probably result in frostbite, because unlike him, I don't have gloves. I must admit—the man came more prepared than I did.

'I'm a bit cold,' I reply. 'My boots aren't snow proof.'

Ethan looks down at his own footwear, then back up at me. After a moment of consideration, he tromps around the side of the car, then crouches down beside me. 'Okay, hop on my back.'

Forget everything I said. I love my husband. Truly.

He gives me a piggyback ride along the rest of the path, past the FOR SALE sign on the snow-covered front lawn, and all the way to the front door. The porch has been largely shielded from the snow, and that's where he carefully lowers me onto the ground. He shakes snow-flakes out of his now damp blonde hair and blinks droplets of water from his eyelashes.

'Thank you.' I smile at him, giddy with affection for my strong, handsome husband. 'You're my hero.'

'My pleasure.' And then he bows. *Swoon*. I'm loving this honeymoon phase of our marriage.

Ethan pulls off his wool gloves and presses his thumb against the doorbell. We hear the chimes ringing out throughout the house, but after several moments of waiting, no footsteps are coming to the door to let us in.

The other strange thing is that the first floor of the house is completely dark. We both saw that light on upstairs, so we assumed someone was home. We assumed it was Judy. But if Judy were here, she would be downstairs, wouldn't she? She wouldn't be upstairs in a random bedroom. The first floor of the house is dead silent.

'Maybe the owners are home,' Ethan says, straining his neck to look up at the towering estate.

'Maybe …'

But there's another strange thing about all this. There's no car on the property. Not that I can see anyway. Of course, in a snowstorm, the owner's car would likely be tucked away in the garage. Judy likely wouldn't park in the garage, so the fact that her car isn't visible is evidence that she hasn't arrived.

Ethan rings the doorbell again while I pull my phone out of my purse. 'There are no messages from Judy,' I report. 'Although my signal went out at least twenty minutes ago, so it's possible she's trying to contact us now.'

He digs his own phone out of his pocket and frowns down at the screen. 'I don't have any signal either.'

We still hear only silence coming from the house. Ethan walks over to the window next to the door and cups his hands over his eyes to see inside. He shakes his head.

'There definitely isn't anybody on the first floor. I'm not convinced there's anyone here at all.' He shrugs. 'Maybe Judy left the light on upstairs the last time she was here.'

That doesn't sound like Judy. Judy Teitelbaum is the consummate professional. She's been showing houses since before I was born, and every place she has shown us has been immaculate. She must scrub them down herself.

I'm afraid to even touch anything when I'm in one of the houses for a showing. If I put down a drink without a coaster, I might give Judy a stroke. So no, I don't think she would leave the house with an upstairs light on. But I'm struggling to come up with another explanation.

Ethan tugs at the collar of his puffy jacket while I hug myself for warmth. 'Well, I don't know what to do. She's obviously not here.'

I let out a frustrated sigh. 'Great. So what are we supposed to do?'

'Hang on.' His eyes drop to the mat below our feet—the word 'Welcome' is written in elaborate script, partially obscured by the snow. 'Maybe there's a spare key around here somewhere.'

There isn't one under the welcome mat—that would be far too obvious—but a more thorough search turns up a key concealed beneath a potted plant near the door. The key is ice cold and slightly damp in my palm.

'So …' I raise my eyebrows at Ethan. 'Should we go inside without her? Do you think that's okay?'

'We better. Who knows how long she's going to be, and it's freezing out here.' He throws an arm protectively around my shoulders. 'I don't want you to catch pneumonia.'

He's right. With no cell phone signal and with the car getting increasingly buried in the snow, we need shelter. At least in the house, we'll be safe.

I fit the key in the lock and hear it turn. I place my hand on the doorknob, which is freezing cold under my palm. I attempt to twist the knob, but the door doesn't budge. Damn. I look down at the key, still wedged in the lock. 'Do you think there's a dead bolt?'

'Let me try.'

I step back to let Ethan have a go at it. He jiggles the key a bit, then he tries the knob. Nothing. He steps back for a moment, then grips the doorknob again and throws his entire weight against the heavy wooden door. With a loud creaking sound, the door pops open.

'You did it!' *My hero. Swoon.*

The house is pitch-black inside. Ethan flicks a switch on the wall, and my stomach sinks when nothing happens. But then the overhead lights flicker for a moment before coming to life. The power is on, thank God. The lighting is dim—several of the bulbs have probably blown out—but it's enough to illuminate the expansive living space.

And my jaw drops.

First of all, the living room is huge, and it seems even larger with the open floor plan. After living in a Manhattan apartment for the last several years, almost every house seems enormous to us. But this one is *museum*-level enormous. It's *airport*-level enormous. And as large as the square footage is, it seems so much larger because of the high ceilings.

'Jesus,' Ethan breathes. 'This place is incredible. It's like a cathedral.'

'Yes.'

'And the asking price is so *low*. This house looks like it should be worth four times as much as that.'

Even as I nod my head in agreement with him, I get another wave of that sick feeling. *Something terrible has happened in this house.*

'There could be mold,' he says thoughtfully. 'Or the foundation is crap. We should have the place inspected by someone really good before we sign anything.'

I don't respond to that. I don't tell him I'm secretly hoping this place is infested with mold or crumbling at the base or that there's some other reason that I can say no to living here without sounding like an unreasonable woman who won't buy a house her husband loves because she has *a bad feeling* about it.

And there's something else strange about this house.

It's completely furnished. The living room has a sectional sofa, a love seat, a coffee table, and bookcases overflowing with books. I walk over to the beautiful brown leather sectional sofa and run my finger along one of the cushions. The leather feels stiff, like nobody has used the cushions in ages, and my finger comes away black. Dust— years' worth of it.

Some of the houses we've seen have been furnished because the owners were still living there, but those houses looked lived in. This house doesn't. There is a thick layer of dust on every piece of furniture in the living room. Yet this furniture isn't the kind that somebody would leave behind when they moved. That leather couch probably cost somewhere in the order of five figures. And who leaves behind every single one of their books?

The floor looks dusty too, like nobody has walked on it in a long time. When I raise my eyes,

I notice thick cobwebs in every corner of the living room. I can almost imagine the spiders crawling through those webs, waiting to sink their fangs into me.

It's also more evidence that Judy has not been here. There's no way Judy would leave a house this dusty. And cobwebs? Not a chance. It's against her religion.

I turn to Ethan, about to point this out, but he's distracted by something. A gigantic portrait of a woman hanging over the mantel. He is staring up at it, a strangely dark look on his face.

'Hey,' I say. 'What's wrong?'

His pale eyelashes flutter. He seems surprised that I'm suddenly standing next to him, as if he had forgotten I was here. 'Oh. Uh, nothing. I just … Who do you think that is?' I follow his gaze up to the portrait. It's gigantic— larger than life. And the woman featured in the portrait is striking. There's no other word for her— she's the sort of woman who, if you saw her on the street, you would stop and do a double take. She looks to be in her mid-thirties, with pin-straight hair that falls just below her shoulders. At first, I would have called her hair auburn, but when I tilt my head to the side, it morphs into a brilliant shade of red. Her skin is pale and flawless, but I suppose anyone can have beautiful skin in a painting. One of her most striking features is her vivid green eyes. So many people have green eyes flecked with brown or blue, but hers are such an intense shade of green that they seem like they could leap off the canvas.

'Maybe she lived here?' I suggest.

Ethan's lips twist into a sneer. 'What kind of arrogant, self-obsessed person would put a gigantic painting of herself over the fireplace?'

'You mean you don't want me to put a giant painting of myself on the wall in our new home?' I tease him.

Ethan flashes me a withering smile. Something about the painting has disturbed him, and he doesn't seem like he wants to talk about it.

I wander over to the bookcase near the fireplace, still wearing my wool coat because it's far too cold to remove it. Whoever lived here must've loved to read, because there are multiple bookcases scattered throughout the room, all nearly overflowing with books. I glance at some titles on the shelves, in case we are stuck here for a while and I need something to entertain me. There's an entire shelf containing books with the exact same title.

The Anatomy of Fear.

A little shiver goes down my spine, and I hug my coat to my chest. I pluck one of the many hardcover titles off the shelf, which has a layer of dust on it, like everything else in the house. *The Anatomy of Fear* by Adrienne Hale, MD, PhD. And there's a picture of a dripping knife on the cover. Great. Exactly what I want to see right now.

I flip the book around. There are a few choice quotes from well known authors and professionals praising the book. And in the left-hand lower corner, there's a photograph of the author. It's the same picture that's hanging over the mantel.

'Ethan,' I say. 'Look at this.'

He rips his eyes away from the portrait and joins me by the bookcase. He looks over my shoulder at the photograph on the back of the book. 'Adrienne Hale,' he reads off the back cover. 'Isn't she that shrink who got murdered?'

He's right. Three years ago, the disappearance of Dr Adrienne Hale was one of the biggest stories in the news. Especially since it happened shortly after the release of her pop psychology hit, which stayed on the *New York Times* bestseller list for almost a year, hogging the number one spot for months. Everyone in the country read that book, including yours truly. Of course, the massive success of the book was largely because her disappearance was such a sensational story.

'She disappeared,' I correct him. 'I don't think they ever found her body.'

He tugs the hardcover out of my hands and flips through the pages. 'I bet they did eventually find her. Washed up somewhere.'

'Maybe.' Adrienne Hale disappeared from the news cycle at least two years ago, and her book dropped off the charts as well. 'You read it, didn't you?'

His eyes are still on the pages in front of him as he shakes his head. 'I hate that pop psychology crap.'

'No, it was really good.' I poke a finger at the open pages in his hand. 'It's all about her patients, you know? The horrible experiences they went through and how they dealt with it.'

'Yeah, not interested.' He rests the book on top of a random shelf, suddenly bored with it. Ethan isn't much of a reader. 'Her boyfriend killed her, right? I remember that part. He was some tech guy or something.'

'They accused him but I don't think he went to jail for it.'

'He probably did it though.'

'Probably.' I nod. 'There are a lot of dangerous men out there.'

He grabs my hand and pulls me toward him so I can feel his hot breath on my cheek. 'Aren't you glad I saved you from all those jerks?'

I roll my eyes, but he's not entirely wrong. I've dated some jerks in the past. Nobody who was homicidal like Dr Adrienne Hale's boyfriend, but I had a guy once cheat on me with my best friend. It was almost a cliché. Ethan, on the other hand, has been incredibly loyal during the time we've been together. He never even looks at other women, even though they look at him all the time.

'You think this is her house then?' I ask. 'Dr Adrienne Hale?'

'Probably.' He glances up at the portrait again. 'That or somebody who was dangerously obsessed with her.'

Even though I'm wearing my coat, I'm still freezing. I rub my arms for warmth. If we're here much longer, maybe we can figure out how to turn on the heat. Ethan is good at stuff like that. 'Wouldn't it bother you to live in the home of a dead woman?'

'Not really.' He shrugs. 'Everyone dies eventually, right? So unless we buy a brand-new house, you're kind of guaranteed somebody has lived in it who's now dead. So what?'

Fun new facts I'm learning about my husband of six months: he does *not* have a spiritual side.

My gaze skims over the contents of the bookcase, resting on the book Ethan casually tossed on top of the shelf. Somehow, it feels like Adrienne Hale wouldn't like him messing with her bookshelf—like he disturbed the energy in the house. I take the book and replace it on the shelf where it was before. Hopefully that appeases her ghost temporarily, even if her killer is still out there somewhere.

My stomach lets out an embarrassing growl. 'When do you think Judy will be here? I'm starving.'

'I have no idea.' He looks down at his Rolex. 'Let me double-check if her car is in the garage.'

While Ethan goes off in search of the door to the garage, my gaze drops to the floor beneath my feet. The wood is so filthy that I'd be reluctant to walk barefoot here—the soles of my feet would almost certainly turn black. But as I look down at the floor in the flickering light from the overhead lamps, I notice a change in the dust pattern near the bookcase. It almost looks like …

A footprint.

I creep over to get a closer look, squinting in the dim lighting. It definitely looks like a footprint. I put my own boot next to the print—whoever made the footprint had feet quite a lot larger than mine. Could it be Ethan's foot-print? It looks about the right size, but I didn't see him standing over here.

'The garage is empty.' Ethan emerges from a door near the kitchen, brushing what looks like a cobweb off his shoulder. 'Judy's not here.'

I shiver, even with my coat still on. 'Hey, come look at this.'

Ethan walks over to me, and I recognize that the two of us are creating new footprints everywhere we go. 'What? What's wrong?'

'Is this a footprint?'

He narrows his eyes at the dust pattern on the floor. 'Maybe?'

'So who made it?'

'I don't know. Judy?'

I raise my eyebrows. 'You think Judy wears size-ten men's shoes?'

Ethan lets out a breath, and I swear I can see the puff of air in the frigid living room. 'Then maybe it was someone else viewing the house.'

Except there's no way Judy was showing anyone a house this dusty. My eyes scan the floor, but I don't see any other footprints as noticeable as these. 'When do you think Judy will get here?'

He frowns. 'I don't know if Judy is going to make it, Tricia.'

'She wouldn't stand us up.'

'Yeah, but there's a blizzard out there. We barely made it, and the snow is just getting worse. Honestly, it was irresponsible of her to even schedule the viewing tonight.'

'So …' I chew on the tip of my thumbnail. 'Do you think we could be stuck here? Like, for the night?'

Our heads swivel simultaneously to look over at one of the picture windows. The snow is coming down harder than it's ever been before. It's like a wall of white is being dumped from the sky. Our car is probably buried, and it's not like it was doing so great in the snow before.

'I think we might be,' he says. 'But don't worry. I mean, look at this place—I bet the kitchen is stocked with food. And even if it isn't, we've got that emergency supply kit you make me keep in the trunk. Doesn't that have a bunch of power bars in it?'

'I ... I think so ...'

'So let's go get something to eat.'

Ethan strides purposefully in the direction of the kitchen. I can't believe he's not even the slightest bit worried, even though we're now trapped in this unfamiliar house full of cobwebs and scary footprints. That's how Ethan is. He's always so confident. I love that about him. So I follow my new husband to the kitchen. But the whole time, I can't shake the horrible feeling that those green eyes in the portrait over the mantel are watching me.

CHAPTER 3

ADRIENNE

BEFORE

Paige is cursing to herself as she stumbles on a loose brick on the walkway to my front door. I watch her from the window, wondering if I should call someone to get that brick fixed this week. I don't want somebody to fall on it, shatter their ankle, and then I'm responsible. Legally, that is. If Paige fell, it would be her own fault. She would have far more stability if she weren't clutching a manila enve-lope in her right hand and scrolling through her phone with her left as she teeters in her three-inch heels.

Paige has been my literary agent for the last five years, and I have never seen her without her phone in hand. There's a possibility it has fused to her palm. I have spoken to her in the past and I swear I've heard the shower running in the background. Once, I heard the toilet flush. When we speak, she looks up from the screen to meet my eyes, but only briefly.

Paige tucks the manila envelope under her arm so she can ring the doorbell. It's unnecessary, given I've been monitoring her Audi's trajectory down my driveway, but she doesn't know that. Chimes echo through the house, and I take my time heading to the front door. Paige may be in a rush, but I'm not. I've got the entire morning free before my first patient arrives.

Paige has her eyes pinned on her phone screen when I crack open the door. Her usually perfectly highlighted hair is slightly windblown from the drive, but she otherwise looks impeccable in a black silk dress and spiky pumps.

'Adrienne!' A smile spreads across my agent's face at the sight of me, although she still doesn't put away her phone. 'How are you?'

How are you? The three most useless words in the universe of communication. Nobody who asks that question wants to know the answer. And nobody who answers ever tells the truth. 'I'm fine, Paige.'

She pauses for a beat, waiting for me to return the nicety. When it is obvious that I'm not going to, she shakes her phone slightly in her left hand. 'Sorry I was late. The GPS conked out on my phone. The signal around here is terrible.'

'Yes,' I say sympathetically. 'It is.'

I live far enough off the beaten path that most people can't get a signal out here. Within my house, I have a MicroCell tower and Wi-Fi. But in anticipation of Paige's visit, I shut them both off. While she is here, I want her full attention. I would never pay more attention to my phone than to a patient, and I don't enjoy competing for Paige's attention.

I take a step back to allow Paige to enter the house. She's only been here once before, and she sucks in a breath at the sheer size of it all. The living area is impressive. Paige lives in Manhattan, probably in a tiny shoebox of an apartment that costs a small fortune.

'This is an amazing house,' she breathes. She is so astounded that she lowers her phone entirely so that it hangs at her side. 'So much space.'

'Thank you.'

Her eyes dart around, from the sectional leather sofa to the antique bookcases to the spiraling staircase up to the second level. She could just leave the compliment as it is, but that's not Paige's style. Instead, she feels compelled to add, 'It's just you in this big place?'

She knows I'm not married. No children. My parents are long gone. 'Yes. Just me.'

'Geez …' She scratches her cheek. 'I'd be scared to live here. I mean, you *are* out in the middle of nowhere. You don't even have good cell service. Anyone could come in here and …'

It's not as if Paige is the first person to suggest such a thing. If I had any close family members or close friends, I'm sure they would worry about me. But I'm not worried.

'Do you have a security system?' she asks.

I lift a shoulder. 'I have locks on the doors.'

She looks at me like I've lost my mind. But I feel safe here. Isolation is not necessarily dangerous. The turn to get onto the small dirt road to my house is so narrow that many people drive by it without even noticing. And I need the extra space because this house also serves as my office. I do my writing here, and I have a room where I see patients.

I'm disappointed in Paige for her judgment, even though I'm not surprised. I'm sure many people could judge her for her own choices. If she hadn't taken the time to push out two rug rats, she might be further in her career. She might not have to suck up to someone like me. And also, she wears far too much makeup. I don't trust women who cake on layers of foundation like a mask that adheres directly to their skin.

'You know …' Paige gives a sympathetic tilt of her head. 'I could see if Alex knows anyone for you. I'm sure one of his colleagues from work would be happy to take you out.'

'No need,' I say through my teeth. 'Are you sure? Because—'

'I'm sure.'

She shrugs like she thinks I have made a tragic error in judgment by not accepting a pity date from her husband. It's not the first time she's offered. After a few times, you would think she'd get the message I'm not interested, but sadly, she has not.

'Anyway.' Paige thrusts the manila envelope at me, her bright red fingernails shining under the overhead lights. 'Here's the proof of your new book.'

I accept the envelope from her grasp. I'm tempted to rip it open. This book is the culmination of two years of research and late nights spent poring over my notes and pounding on the keyboard. But I don't want to look at it in front of Paige. I'll do it after she leaves.

'Thank you,' I say.

'Gruesome stuff,' she comments, crinkling her nose. She made no secret of the fact that she thought I should 'tone down' some of the violent scenes described in the book, but I was adamant they should stay as is. 'It's hard to read—for some people.'

'It's all true.'

Paige eyes the envelope in my hand. She was hoping I would open it in front of her. She drove all the way up here from Manhattan after all. It's no small trip to Westchester, but my first book, *Know Yourself*, was on the *New York Times* bestseller list for twenty-seven weeks. This highly anticipated follow-up could be worth a fortune to her. She wants to keep me happy.

She stands there for a moment, waiting to see if I'll offer her a tour or perhaps a cup of coffee. She wants to be my friend. Or at least she wants a pretend friendship where we gossip, do lunch at a café, and act as though we don't dislike one another.

I don't have friends. I never have.

'Could I ...' She licks her lips. 'Could I trouble you for a glass of water?'

I throw a glance toward my kitchen. 'Of course. The water is a bit brown though, I have to warn you. I've gotten used to the metallic taste, but it bothers some people.'

Her nose crinkles again. She has the faintest hint of freckles on the bridge, no doubt covered by several layers of makeup. 'Brown water? Adrienne, you should have somebody take a look at that.'

'Oh, I don't mind. It tastes fine. Let me grab that water for you.'

'Actually, that's okay.'

'Are you sure?'

'Yes, it's fine.' She looks a tad green at the idea of choking down a glass of my fictional brown water. She wants to be my friend, but not that badly. 'I should be heading out now. It's a long drive back to the city.'

I nod. 'Drive safely.'

She takes one last long look around my house. She's probably wondering how much it cost me. In another life, Paige could have been a real estate agent. She has the right personality for it. Pushy as hell.

'Honestly,' she says, 'you should think about getting some sort of security system for this place. I don't want to come here one day and find you murdered in the living room.'

Statistically, the risk of such a thing is low. Less than a quarter of all homicide victims are female. Most of those women are young and low-income.

'Or get a boyfriend,' Paige adds with a laugh. 'Like I said, happy to help on that front.'

Up to 70 per cent of females who have been murdered were killed by an intimate partner. So in actuality, her sug-gestion to 'get a boyfriend' is not only highly judgmental and insulting but would only *increase* my risk of meeting with a violent end. But I will not debate this woman.

'I'm really fine,' I say again. 'I don't need a security system.'

She considers this for a moment, then snorts. 'Yeah, that's right. You invite the crazies right in, don't you?'

It hits me now. I don't know how I never saw it. Paige doesn't respect what I do. She has been my advocate through two publications, and in her defense, she's damn good at it. But she doesn't believe in any of it. To her, the people I help are a bunch of 'crazies.'

During the five years I have known Paige, she has insulted my home and my lifestyle choices, and she's been the harshest critic of my manuscripts. I have taken every bit of her abuse because she's good at what she does. But today, she has crossed a line.

Nobody talks about my patients that way.

'Paige.' I tap the corner of my right eye. 'You've got a bit of mascara caked right here.'

'Oh!' Her black eyelashes flutter as her hand flies self-consciously to her eyes. She automatically reaches into her purse to search for a compact, but in the process, her phone slips from her left hand and clatters loudly to the wood floor. 'Shit …'

She scoops up her phone—there's a spiderweb of cracks imprinted on the screen. She looks like she's going to burst into tears.

'Oh dear,' I say. 'It looks like your phone got cracked.'

'Shit.' She runs her index finger over the screen as if she might magically fix it with her touch. She swears again and yanks her finger away. The glass has sliced right through the pad of her finger. 'Just my luck, right?'

'Maybe it's a sign,' I say. 'Perhaps you should spend less time on your phone.'

Paige laughs like I made a joke. She doesn't know me well enough to know that I don't make jokes.

Her smile is strained as I lead her to the door, and once she gets outside, the smile drops off her face altogether. I watch from the window as she makes her way back to her car, this time avoiding the treacherous loose brick. As soon as she slides into the driver's seat, she twists her body to look at her reflection in the rearview mirror. She touches the corner of her eye, frowning as she searches for the mascara I had assured her was caked in there.

She's having a bad day. But it's going to get much worse when she gets the email from me terminating her as my agent.

I turn away from the window and look down at the manila envelope that Paige left me. My book. Two years of blood, sweat, and tears.

I carefully lift the clasp and open the envelope. I pull the proof copy of my book from within. The corners of my lips twitch. The book is exactly the way I envisioned it. My name is in bold block letters: Adrienne Hale, MD, PhD. The publisher balked when I suggested the knife dripping with blood on the book cover, but after the success of my last book, I got to call the shots. They must realize now what a brilliant decision it was—how striking the image is. I trace the letters of the title as I read the words out loud:

The Anatomy of Fear.

CHAPTER 4

TRICIA

PRESENT DAY

I don't have much hope for the kitchen. If this house hasn't been lived in during the three years Adrienne Hale has been missing, how can there be any food in the refrigerator? The best we can hope for is some stuff in cans that we can heat up.

The refrigerator is at least twice the size of the tiny one we have stuffed into our kitchen at home. Everything here seems to be orders of magnitude larger than what we have back in the city. About ten copies of our kitchen could fit into this one. I wonder if Dr Adrienne Hale was a skilled chef. She seems like the sort of woman who could whip up a gourmet meal.

Ethan throws open the refrigerator and peers inside. 'Well, we can make ourselves sandwiches.'

'Really?' I look over his shoulder into the fridge. There's a loaf of bread in there and a bunch of cold cuts. There's even a jar of mayonnaise. My stomach turns and

I almost gag thinking about how long that food has been sitting in there. 'I'm not eating that. It probably expired years ago.'

He picks up a packet of bologna. 'Nope. It doesn't expire for another week. Judy must have bought it.'

I try to imagine Judy purchasing a packet of bologna for one of the houses she is showing. I can't seem to do it. She's more of a caviar-and-smoked-salmon type of person. 'Are you sure? Are you looking at the *year*?'

'*Yes*. Here, look.'

He hands me the bologna. Sure enough, the date on it is for the current year, one week in the future. I open it up and sniff it, and it doesn't smell rancid. The colour looks okay.

'I'll make us sandwiches,' he says.

Ethan lines up a loaf of bread, the bologna, and a jar of mayonnaise on the counter, and he gets to work making us sandwiches. He likes to cook for me. It's sweet. Not that I can't make a simple sandwich on my own, but it's romantic the way he enjoys pampering me. Yet another thing I've quickly learned to love about him.

I just hope he feels the same way about me after he finds out about my revelation. I feel ill every time I think about it. But I can't keep it from him much longer.

'Is there anything I can do?' I ask.

'Why don't you grab us something to drink?'

I can handle that. I walk to the other side of the kitchen to find a couple of glasses. I'll just fill them up with tap water—I'm sure it's fine. But when I get close to the sink, something makes me stop in my tracks.

It's a cup right by the sink. Half filled with water. The outside dripping with condensation.

'Ethan?' My voice sounds shaky.

'Yeah?'

'I ...' I swallow as my eyes stay on the glass. 'I think there's somebody else in this house.'

His head snaps up from the sandwich preparation. He's got a slice of bologna clutched in his right hand. 'What are you talking about?'

'There's a cup here.' I back away for a minute, like the cup might reach out and strangle me. 'Somebody filled it recently and was drinking from it.'

'Probably Judy.'

If he mentions Judy again, I'm going to punch him in the face. 'It's not Judy's, okay? Judy would never leave half a glass of water on the kitchen counter like this. And if she did, there'd be lipstick all over the rim.'

He can't argue with that. Judy's trademark is her bright red lipstick. She would never be able to drink from a glass without a little bit of it wiping off.

'And I saw that footprint on the floor,' I remind him. 'That was probably Judy's,' he says, even though it's preposterous. 'Or mine.'

'Also,' I add, 'we saw that light on upstairs when we were walking over here. Somebody is upstairs.'

Ethan purses his lips. He looks over at the water glass across the kitchen, then up at the spiral staircase leading to the second floor. 'I don't know, Tricia. If someone else were here, wouldn't they have come down and told us to get the hell out of their house?'

He has a good point. 'Maybe they're not supposed to be here.'

He doesn't disregard the possibility. Now his eyes are trained on the stairwell. 'Okay. Suppose that's true. What should we do?'

I've still got my purse slung over my shoulder. I reach inside and pull out my phone. Still no signal. 'I think we should check upstairs.' Ethan looks like he's about to protest, so I quickly add, 'We're stuck here for the night. Are *you* going to be able to sleep if you know a stranger is lurking around the house?'

'You're right,' Ethan finally says. 'I should go check it out. You stay here.'

'No way.' I shake my head vigorously. 'I'm going with you. You're *not* leaving me alone down here.'

Again, he seems like he's about to protest but then thinks better of it. He rubs his chin with his thumb for a moment, then reaches for something on the kitchen counter. It takes me a moment to realize that it's a block of knives. The long-serrated blade Ethan pulls out glints in the light from the overhead lamps in the kitchen. 'Should be prepared, right?'

I have no objection to him taking a knife. I'm tempted to grab one myself.

We walk together across the living room, past the portrait of Dr Adrienne Hale. I'm quickly starting to despise that painting. This house is creepy enough without those green eyes following me around everywhere. It's a relief when we get to the staircase, away from her gaze.

At least it's a relief until we start climbing. The stairs wind up for what feels like an eternity, and the stairwell is very dark. The stairs are steep, and each one creaks as our feet put weight on it—the sound echoes through the entire stairwell. I cling to the ornate wooden banister with one hand, and with the other, I reach out for my husband. When I find his arm, I grab on to it tightly. I can't believe he wants to *live* here. This place feels like a haunted house we're forced to spend the night in to earn some sort of inheritance or something like that.

The worst part is when we get to the landing for the second floor. Because it's obvious that the entire floor is completely dark.

'We saw a light on up here, right?' My eyes frantically dart between the doorways, each darker than the next. 'I'm sure we did.'

'Maybe it was the moonlight reflecting on the window.'

I glare at him in the dim light from the window. 'So the moon somehow reflected on only *one* bedroom window?'

'I don't know what to tell you, Tricia. I don't see anyone up here. And all the lights are out.'

'Shouldn't we check the rooms?'

He's quiet for a moment. I can't tell whether he's scared or annoyed. 'Fine. Let's check the bedrooms.'

Ethan flips on the light in the hallway, which is burned out except for one single bulb. But even that is enough to make the second floor a lot less scary. He keeps the knife down at his side as we open each room and turn on the light. According to the description on Judy's website, there are six bedrooms upstairs, and I'm not leaving here until we check every single one of them.

First bedroom—empty.

Same deal for the second, third, and fourth bedrooms.

All of them are completely dark and quiet. When Ethan turns on the lights, nobody is lurking in the shadows. Each room is completely empty.

'I don't think there's anyone here, Tricia,' he says as he closes the door of the fourth bedroom.

'Keep looking,' I say through my teeth. Fifth bedroom—empty.

Now there's one last room left. All the bedrooms we have seen so far have been about the same size and rather impersonal looking. This leads me to suspect that the last bedroom must be the master bedroom. The place where Adrienne Hale slept every night in the months and years before her disappearance.

As we walk to the final door, I grab on to Ethan's arm.

My heart is pounding so hard that it hurts my chest.

'Tricia, your nails ...'

I ease up my grip ever so slightly. 'Sorry.'

I'm probably still gouging him with my nails, but he lets me do it. He lowers the hand not clutching the knife onto the doorknob. And quietly, he twists the knob.

CHAPTER 5

'There's no one here,' Ethan announces.

He flips the switch inside the last room, setting the space aglow. This room is significantly larger than all the others and looks like it's a master bedroom. There's a king-size bed in the centre of the room with an ornate wooden headboard. The bed is made up, and when I reach out a finger to touch the cream-coloured bedspread with the red trim, it too has a thick layer of dust on it.

'Nobody.' He taps open the bathroom door and peeks inside. 'Not even hiding in the bathroom.'

'I can see that.'

He fiddles with the handle of the knife. 'So are you satisfied? Or do you want me to check under the bed?'

I don't need him to check under the bed, but it wouldn't be a terrible idea to check the closet. I grab the shiny gold handle of a door near the bathroom and fling it open. It is, as I suspected, a walk-in closet. That's another luxury we don't have in our Manhattan apartment.

Rows of expensive-looking clothing line the expansive closet—I see tags from Gucci, Louis Vuitton, and Versace. And there's just a hint of a sweet-smelling perfume enclosed in the closet, like a tomb—Chanel, I think. I run my fingers over the fabric of a white sweater hanging there—cashmere.

This, more than anything, is evidence that Dr Adrienne Hale is dead. Because no woman would voluntarily leave here without taking this gorgeous sweater with her.

'Satisfied, Tricia?'

I pull my fingers away from the cashmere sweater. 'I don't get it. Why was the light on?'

'Maybe it was a bulb that blew out?'

I shake my head. 'It couldn't be. We turned on all the overhead lights, and they all work perfectly.'

'Maybe it was a lamp.'

I shoot him a look.

Ethan throws up his hands. 'I don't know what you want me to tell you. We checked every room. We've looked in the closet. *There's nobody here.*'

I can't argue with him. He's right that we have checked every room and looked as carefully as we can. If there's someone here, they don't want us to find them. Maybe it's better if we don't find them.

'Fine,' I say. 'Let's go have dinner.'

Except if we sleep in one of the bedrooms tonight, I am definitely locking the door. And barricading it.

As we walk back down the spiraling stairs to the first floor, I don't feel much better about anything. In fact, I feel more anxious. I'm certain I saw the light on from outside the house, and the fact that none of those lights are on is deeply unsettling. I don't know why Ethan doesn't seem upset about it. Maybe he's just hiding it well.

After we get back downstairs, I notice a room off to the side with the door cracked open right by the stairwell. I tap on the door to push it the rest of the way open, and I gasp slightly. Ethan freezes in his steps.

'What's wrong?' he asks.

I peer inside this new room. Like many of the rooms in the house, it's huge. And like the living room, the walls are lined with bookcases, all stuffed with books. I don't think I've ever seen this many books in my life. By the window in the corner is a large mahogany desk, with a leather chair behind it and a dusty desktop computer sit-ting on top. The final piece of furniture in the room is a large leather sofa. Dr Adrienne Hale clearly loved leather furnishings.

'This must have been her office,' I breathe.

Ethan glances around, an appreciative look on his face. 'When we live here, I could use this room for *my* office.'

'Uh …' I don't want to burst his bubble and tell him that at the moment, there's no way in hell I'm willing to consider living in this house. If only because I will forever be terrified that there is a stranger hidden in one of the dark recesses of the second floor. 'Sure.'

'I'd hardly have to change a thing.' He presses a hand against the sofa, testing its integrity. 'Well, I'd get rid of all the books. But other than that, it's perfect.'

'Yes. Perfect.' Over my dead body.

Ethan leans in to plant a kiss on my cheek. 'I'm going to finish making our sandwiches. You can browse her library.'

Before I have a chance to protest, Ethan has left to return to the kitchen. I want to follow him, but my legs feel frozen. This office. Even more than the rest of the house, it gives me the creeps.

This is where she worked. She was almost certainly in this room on the day she disappeared. Even more than the master bedroom, this room feels haunted by her presence. I walk over to the mahogany desk. This room is dusty, but not as bad as the living room. There's just a thin layer of dust over the desk and the computer keys. I pluck a tissue out of a box she has on the desk and run it over the black computer monitor. Then I dust off the seat of the leather chair.

I settle down in the chair, and it creaks threateningly under my weight. Is this where Dr Hale wrote *The Anatomy of Fear*? For a while, it seemed like everybody in the country had read that book. It was the 'it' book. And she never got to enjoy it because soon after it was released, she vanished into thin air.

I study the contents of the desk. She's got a pencil holder in the shape of a human brain, loaded up with ballpoint pens. Her keyboard is one of those ergonomic ones, curved so that her hands could lie at a more natural position. And there's another object on the desk that gets my attention.

It's a tape recorder.

I haven't seen a tape recorder in many years. I vaguely remember my parents having one when I was a little girl, but that's it. It's an outdated piece of technology. I blow the dust off the recorder and pick it up, curious to see what Dr Hale had been listening to before her disappearance.

But it's empty. Of course, the police would have taken whatever tape was inside as evidence.

'Tricia! Sandwiches are ready!'

Ethan's voice floats down the hallway into the office. I lower the tape recorder back onto the desk and leave the office to join him.

CHAPTER 6

ADRIENNE

BEFORE

It is extremely rare for mental-health workers to be killed by patients.

It happens about once a year in this country. In most instances, the victims are young female caseworkers. The homicides most frequently occur while the victims are visiting residential treatment facilities. And the most likely perpetrators are males with schizophrenia.

The majority of victims are killed by gunshot wounds. Not that a psychiatrist who rarely sees inpatients is immune from such an attack. At any moment during a session, my patients could stand up, grab the letter opener off my desk, and jam it through my eye socket. But my risk is relatively low. Even though I see patients in my home, which people tell me is a mistake, I feel safe.

Also, I don't actually keep a letter opener on my desk. That would be tempting fate.

And I take one other precaution. Every single patient I accept for treatment is vetted by me personally. I refuse to accept any patients with whom I do not feel comfortable.

With one exception. But that will resolve itself soon enough.

Right now, my mind isn't on my patients as I sit at my computer, replying to messages via email. I'm currently composing a reply to a message I received yesterday from my former agent, Paige.

Dear Adrienne,

I was shocked and saddened to hear that you wanted to work with another agent at the company for your next project. In addition to being an incredible writer, I have considered you one of my closest friends. I have worked extremely hard nurturing your talent these past years. Can you please let me know what I have done to offend you and I'll do whatever I can to make it right?

Your friend,
Paige

It takes all my self-restraint not to roll my eyes at Paige's email. She and I are not friends. Not even close. I am a trained psychiatrist and psychotherapist. Does she honestly believe that her insincere flattery and overfamiliarity will endear her to me? And how exactly has she *nurtured* my talent aside from taking 15 per cent of everything I've made? But the best part of being a bestselling author is that I don't have to answer to people like Paige. I get to call the shots—and my contract is with the agency, not with Paige herself. So my reply to my former agent is extremely succinct.

> *Paige,*
>
> *I'm afraid that I just don't feel that you are a good fit for me any more. Best of luck to you.*
>
> *Sincerely,*
> *Adrienne Hale, MD, PhD*

As I hit Send on the email, I wonder how Paige will respond. Will she accept that I don't want her to be my agent any more and take the rejection gracefully, or will she haul her Audi back out to Westchester and beg on her knees for me to take her back? I suspect it will be the latter. Human beings don't deal well with rejection. Back when our ancestors were hunters and gatherers, being ostracized from a tribe was akin to a death sentence. For that reason, rejection is experienced by human beings as being incredibly painful. Studies using functional MRI have shown the same areas of the brain become activated both during rejection and during real physical pain.

Some people deal with rejection better than others. Paige won't deal with it well. I can already see it unfold. But it doesn't matter. Once I make a decision, I never go back on it.

A new message pops up in my inbox. The sender is a woman named Susan Jamison—a name I am very familiar with. I click on the new message, already aware of what it is likely to say.

Dr Hale,

I appreciate the work you have attempted to do with my son, but I don't feel like he's making any progress. As I told you two months earlier, I will no longer be paying for his sessions. I'm sorry he has not been reimbursing you himself out of his allowance, but I must reiterate that I will no longer be financing any of these therapy sessions. I'm sorry if you assumed otherwise.

Best,
Susan

I look away from the computer screen to the tape recorder sitting on my desk. Ever since I started holding therapy sessions in my home, I have been recording every single one of them. I ask all patients for permission prior to recording the sessions, although even when they tell me no, I still record them.

I find the tape recordings of the therapy sessions to be extremely helpful. Yes, I could take notes as many therapists do, but those could be potentially inaccurate. Tape recordings don't lie.

Right now, I use the tapes to refresh my memory, but I envision that someday, at the end of my career, I might listen to the tapes and write a memoir of my experiences.

But not now. Not for decades. I have many, many years left in my career.

On the cassette case for each patient, I write the patient's initials, the number of the session, and the date.

The case currently lying next to the tape recorder reads 'EJ #136' and then yesterday's date.

EJ is Susan's son. She asked me to work with him about two years ago, stating that he had 'no direction in life.' Within one session, I had diagnosed EJ with narcissistic personality disorder. The characteristics of this diagnosis include a long-term pattern of exaggerated feelings of self-importance, cravings for admiration, and impaired empathy.

I press Play on the tape recorder and listen to the session from yesterday one more time:

'How did your job interview go?'

'Oh, it went great. They loved me. I'm sure they'll be begging me to come work there. But honestly, I don't think I could do it. Everyone at the company seems so stupid. I don't think I could work in a place where I'm surrounded by stupidity all day.' The moment I first met this man, I immediately disliked him. But I had already met Susan and agreed to see her son. I considered telling her no, but I had given her my word. And I did believe that I could help him.

Unfortunately, I do not believe it any longer. I cannot help this man. He has no insight into his shortcomings and he never will. He has no desire to change. And now that his mother is no longer paying me, I have ample excuse to terminate our sessions.

I will never have to see him again.

CHAPTER 7

TRICIA

PRESENT DAY

A bologna sandwich on white bread with mayonnaise is not exactly the best dinner I've ever had in my life, but it fills me up and leaves me feeling only slightly nauseous. Ethan has highbrow taste when it comes to food and always manages to score a table at the trendiest new restaurants, but he demolishes the bologna sandwich without complaint.

'Do you feel better now that you've eaten?' he asks me.

'Yes,' I lie. Eating a cold bologna sandwich hasn't made me forget that there could be a stranger lurking on the second floor of the house.

'Good.' He grabs my hand across the table—mine is freezing but his is surprisingly warm. 'Jesus, Tricia. You're ice cold!'

I don't know what he expects. It's well below freezing outside, and there's no heat in this house. We're both still wearing our coats. 'Yes ...'

'I'll tell you what.' He rises from his chair and automatically grabs both our plates off the table to clear it. His mother taught him well—too bad I never got to meet her. 'Let me figure out the heat. If we've got electricity, I'll bet we can turn the heat on.'

'That would be great.' I grab the two cups of water from the table and follow him to the kitchen, doing my part as well. 'You are the best husband ever.'

Ethan's face lights up. He drops the plates on the kitchen counter and reaches for me. It's awkward since we both have our coats on, but I love how hot his breath is when he kisses me. 'It's easy to be the best husband ever when I have the best wife ever.'

Despite his good looks, Ethan was never much of a ladies' man. The day we met at the coffee shop, I was the one who made the first move. He didn't have many girlfriends before me and doesn't have many friends. Some of my friends warned me it's a red flag, but I'm glad he didn't have a gazillion girlfriends before me or a best buddy to compete with. I always dreamed of being best friends with my husband.

I hope he still feels that way after what I have to tell him this weekend. I have a terrible feeling that the conversation will not go well.

Like everything else in the house, the first-floor bathroom is tucked away and challenging to find. I finally locate it under the spiral staircase. It fills me with the vague concern that if somebody were on the stairs, they could potentially fall through the ceiling of the bathroom. But hopefully the house is better made than that.

The bathroom is large but quaint. The bathtub has feet as well as separate handles for hot and cold water. After I relieve myself, I run a wet piece of toilet paper along the vanity mirror over the sink, cleaning off the dust so that I can see my reflection clearly for the first time since we arrived at this house.

Wow. I don't look so hot.

My hair is blonde with honey highlights and waves courtesy of my curling iron, but right now, it's still damp and dark from the snow, and all the waves have been destroyed—strands are clinging to my skull and my cheeks. My lips are pale, almost blue, and my face is bone white. I grab a tube of lipstick from my purse and apply a healthy coat. There—that's a little better. I try pinching my cheeks to bring back a bit of colour to my face, but it's just making me look blotchy, so I stop.

Anyway, it's just me and Ethan here. Yes, I want to look my best for my husband, but we've been married for six months now. He understands I can't look absolutely perfect all the time. I mean, I'm sure he understands that. Even though he always looks frustratingly perfect.

When I emerge from the bathroom, I notice yet another bookcase tucked behind the stairwell. Geez, Dr Adrienne Hale sure liked books. Most of the bookcases in the house seem to be related to psychiatry or psychology. All stuff about the human mind anyway. But this bookcase is different. This one is filled with paperback novels—guilty pleasures.

I scan the rows of books, searching for something that might entertain me if we're stuck here for much longer. I try to imagine the psychiatrist with the intense green eyes curled up with a Danielle Steel novel—I can't do it. I'm not much of a romance fan either. But she has a few Stephen King novels that are more my speed. And they're long and engaging.

I've already read all the Stephen King books on her shelves, but I wouldn't mind rereading a few classics. And anyway, I won't be here long enough to finish it, so there's no point starting something new. First, I pick up the copy of *It*, but I practically sprain my wrist getting it off the shelf—this one might be a bit long if we're only spending one night. Finally, I decide on *The Shining*—one of my favourites—and I tip the book out to swipe it from the shelf.

Except it doesn't come out.

I pull harder on the book, but only the top of it comes free. The bottom seems wedged in place. And when I move the top of the book, I hear a loud click. And the bookcase shifts slightly.

What the ...?

I glance over my shoulder. Ethan is nowhere in sight. He's probably still fiddling with the heat. I peer around the side of the bookcase—it's shifted away from the wall. I tug on the side of it, and a concealed door swings out toward me. I blink a few times, unable to believe what I'm seeing.

It's a secret room.

CHAPTER 8

The room is completely dark inside, but it feels small. About the size of the walk-in closet upstairs. I squint into the dark space, trying to get my eyes to adjust.

I take another step, and something smacks me in the face. At first, I think it must be a spiderweb, but then I realize it's a cord. I feel around for a moment, trying to grab it. Then my finger makes contact. I tug on the cord, and there's another click as a single bulb illuminates the room.

My eyeballs bulge as I take in the contents of the room. I was right about the small size of the room. Part of me had been scared I might find a dead body stashed in here, but no. The room is filled with more bookcases—wedged into every available space. But these bookcases don't contain books.

They are lined with cassette tapes.

There must be—God, I don't even know—*thousands* of them. And each one is labelled the same way—a set of initials, followed by a number, followed by a date. The dates seem to go back almost ten years, and there are dozens of different initials. The row in front of me is labelled with the initials PL. Those were the same initials of the main subject featured in Dr Hale's smash bestselling book *The Anatomy of Fear*—could it be the same person? Are these tapes PL's private sessions?

And there's one tape that's labelled differently. It's stuck at the end of one of the rows, and all it has is one word in big capital letters:

LUKE

The name jogs my memory slightly. *Luke*. Was that the name of the boyfriend who they thought had killed Adrienne Hale? It was years ago that the whole thing was splashed all over the front page of every newspaper and on every single news channel. *The disappearance of Dr Adrienne Hale*.

I wonder if the police knew about this hidden room.

Vaguely, I hear Ethan calling my name. He's probably got the heater going. I'm sure he's wondering why it's taking me so long in the bathroom. I don't have a reputation for being *quick* in the bathroom, but this is slow, even for me.

'Just a minute!' I yell.

Impulsively, I grab one of the many PL tapes from one of the shelves and stuff it into my coat pocket. Then I yank on the cord hanging from the ceiling, and the room is plunged back into darkness. I step out of the room, and as I shove the bookcase back into place, I hear a reassuring click. When I step back now, I can't tell the hidden room is even there.

I hurry back into the living room, where Ethan is standing in front of the sofa. He's grinning ear to ear, and he's got a bottle of wine dangling from his right hand. 'I got the heat going!'

I shiver. 'It's still freezing in here.'

'Well, it's going to take a little time to heat such a gigantic space.' He nods pointedly at the massive living area. I'd like to point out to him that if we moved in here, our heating bills would be astronomical, but Ethan's got enough family money that he doesn't worry about that sort of stuff. 'Did you find the bathroom all right?'

'Yes.'

I shove my right hand into my deep coat pocket and feel the rectangular shape of the cassette tape. This would be the time to tell him about my discovery. There's no reason not to tell him.

But he won't want me listening to these tapes. He'll tell me it's none of my business—he always complains I'm a huge busybody. I'm not a busybody though—I just have a natural sense of *curiosity*. Is there anything so wrong with that?

'And look!' Ethan holds up the bottle of blood-coloured wine. 'I found something to warm us up in the meantime.'

'Oh?'

He lowers the bottle to read the label. 'It's a cabernet sauvignon. It's from ... Stellenbosch, South Africa.'

'A wine from South Africa?'

'Oh yeah. There are a lot of good cabernets from South Africa.'

Ethan would know. He's something of a wine expert. He can always tell you what regions are the best for what kinds of wine, what sweet or acidic notes to look for in the wine, and what food pairs best with it. Most of the time, I'm just nodding and pretending to know what he's talking about.

'So,' I say, 'you stole a bottle of wine?'

'It's not *great* wine,' he says defensively. I don't know if that's true, although Ethan isn't willing to drink anything cheap, so it must be at least something decent. His favourite wine is Cheval Blanc. 'And anyway, it's Judy's fault for inviting us here in the middle of a blizzard and not even showing up herself. We need something to entertain ourselves.'

'I'm sure Judy didn't realize there was going to be a blizzard,' I say, but it's too late. Ethan is already pouring the wine into two glasses he set up on the coffee table in front of the fireplace.

Ethan sits down on the sectional sofa, and I sit down beside him. He picks up one of the wineglasses, filled almost to the brim with dark red liquid, and I reluctantly do the same. He tilts his glass toward mine.

'To our new home,' he says. Oh God.

Ethan takes a long sip from his wineglass while I contemplate what to do with mine. I can't drink this. Perhaps a sip or two, but not this entire huge glass of wine or anything close to that. And I can't tell Ethan why because he doesn't know that I'm pregnant.

That's right. I'm knocked up.

It's been two weeks since I missed my period. Just a little over a week since I peed on a stick and those two pink lines appeared that would change our entire lives.

I'm terrified to tell him my little secret. Before we got married, we both decided we wanted children. I have a sister, but Ethan is an only child, and his parents have passed on, so we were both on board with the idea of having a family of our own. But—we agreed—no children in the near future. We're relatively young, and we wanted a chance to travel together, to enjoy each other for a couple of years before we brought a baby into the mix. Two years minimum before we even *start* trying—that's what we decided.

Now here I am, six short months after our wedding.

A baby on the way.

It wasn't my fault. I take my birth control pills religiously. I have a timer set to go off on my phone so I don't forget to take it. But I had a respiratory infection last month, and I took some antibiotics for it that they gave me at urgent care. And apparently that made my birth control pills stop working. Who knew?

I am absolutely terrified to tell Ethan. Waiting to have children was something he felt strongly about. He wanted us to have this time to ourselves. I have effectively ruined all his plans. And I'm not sure how he's going to take it. Not well, I assume.

Ethan has a temper. He has never unleashed it on me, but I have observed it in action. He is the CEO of a small startup company that is taking off, and I overheard him once on the phone after one of his employees had screwed something up. My jaw was hanging open at the way he shouted at that poor man on the phone. I had no idea he had it in him. It was a worrying reminder of the fact that I've only known my husband for a little over a year. I don't know yet exactly what he's like.

So I've been carrying around this secret for the last week and a half. I have to tell him soon, but I'm dreading it with every fibre of my being. I don't want him to scream at me like he did at that man on the phone. That will be the official end of our honeymoon.

I wonder if now is the right time. When he's just successfully gotten the heat working, he is excited about the prospect of purchasing this house (even though there's no way we will actually live here), and he's got a glass of wine in his hand. And he's watching me expectantly, to see what I think of the wine.

I should tell him now. It makes sense. But I don't.

Instead, I tip the glass of cabernet back and let it just barely moisten my tongue. Then I lick my lips. 'Mmm. Delicious.'

'Can you taste the menthol note?'

'I … can.'

Ethan takes another long gulp from his wineglass while I take another pretend sip from mine. He reaches for my hand, and I let him take it. 'This is nice,' he sighs.

'Mmm.'

'I can just imagine us living here.' He squeezes my hand as his blue eyes become distant. 'The two of us enjoying a bottle of wine together—a *good* wine—while the fireplace is raging and keeping us warm.'

'And a few kids toddling around,' I add, watching his reaction.

He laughs. 'Maybe in a few years.'

Well, at least he didn't *completely* freak out at the idea of it. I guess it was too much to hope for that I would mention children and he would immediately say, *Yes! I totally changed my mind! Let's get you pregnant right now!*

He scoots closer to me and throws an arm around my shoulders, drawing me closer to him. It gives me an excuse to lower my wineglass onto the coffee table. It really is nice and cozy, snuggled up with him on the couch. Maybe this house isn't so bad. He seems to love it. And if we decide to live here, it will soften the blow of my surprise pregnancy.

But then I glance up at the mantel. To the portrait of Dr Adrienne Hale. It feels like she's staring down at us with those piercing green eyes, her hair a raging fire around her face. I let out a shudder.

'Still cold?' Ethan murmurs into my hair. 'No …'

He follows my gaze to the portrait hanging on the wall. His eyes darken the way they did when he first saw it.

I smile sheepishly. 'Sorry, it's just giving me the creeps.'

'Yeah, I hate it too.' A muscle twitches in his jaw. 'Let me take care of it.'

'What?'

Before I can ask him what he's doing, Ethan has leaped off the couch and is walking purposefully over to the fireplace. He grabs the heavy wooden frame of the portrait and works it loose from the wall. He lowers the painting to the floor, and after a moment of hesitation, he lays it against the wall, facing away from us.

'Ethan.' I squeeze my hands together, which are suddenly sweaty. 'You can't do that.'

'Why not? I'll put it back before we leave. It's not like *she's* going to care.'

I stare at the space over the mantel, unable to articulate the uneasy feeling in the pit of my stomach. Here we are, spending the evening in Dr Adrienne Hale's house, drinking her wine, and now messing with her portrait on the wall. *And* I swiped one of the tapes from her secret room. I don't believe in ghosts, but if I did, her ghost would be *pissed* right now.

But Ethan doesn't seem bothered by it any more, now that he's taken the picture down and it's turned away from us. He sits down beside me again on the sofa and tugs at the top button of my wool coat. 'Think it's warm enough to take this off?'

It has warmed up considerably in the last half hour. I let him undo the buttons on my coat, and after he does that, he kisses my neck. Usually, that's my sweet spot—I go wild. But right now, I feel nothing.

'We should christen our new house,' he murmurs into my neck.

I kiss him back, trying to muster up some enthusiasm as he fumbles with the button on my jeans. But I can't seem to enjoy it like I usually do. Even with the portrait turned around, I still feel Dr Hale's green eyes boring into me.

CHAPTER 9

Well, we do manage to christen the house. It might not be our new house, but we christened *somebody's* house.

Ethan is in a predictably good mood when we're finished. No matter how many times we've had sex, he still acts like it's the greatest thing in the world and he can't believe he got to score with me. It's sweet. He's a sweet guy. My friends were totally wrong about all the red flags. He's not perfect, but who is?

Maybe this is the right time to tell him about the baby. He's in a great mood, he's excited about the house—how can there possibly be a better time?

'You're quiet,' he notes as he zips up his khaki pants.

'Am I?'

'Yeah. You look pensive.'

My lips twitch. 'Pensive?'

'Like you have something on your mind.'

This is the time. I could tell him. Maybe he'll be fine with it. He wants kids *eventually*. No, this isn't quite the schedule we planned. But babies happen. You can't control it.

I open my mouth, ready to say the words. *I'm pregnant, Ethan*. But they don't come out. And I'm not sure why.

Maybe I'm reluctant to give him some surprising and possibly upsetting news when we're stuck in an isolated house, just the two of us, where nobody can hear us and there's no way to leave.

I blink, startled by my thoughts. That last one made no sense at all—it must be some sort of pregnancy hormone paranoia. Yes, I'm worried Ethan won't be thrilled about my news, and yes, he has a temper. But he would *never* hurt me. I know that for a fact.

'I don't have anything on my mind,' I say finally. 'Just a little tired.' I grin at him. 'You wore me out.'

Ethan beams, proud of himself. He stretches so that I can see some golden blonde hairs on his belly. My husband is so handsome. When I first saw him, I thought he was the most perfect-looking man I had ever seen. I figured after I had known him and dated him for a while, I would notice more and more imperfections. And I have identified a few of them. His eyes are too close together. He's a bit on the short side for a man. Those curly golden hairs are not just on his chest but also on his back.

But weirdly, all those imperfections make him even more handsome. I can't explain it.

'Would it bother you if I took a shower?' he asks. 'A shower?'

'Sure. The hot water seems to be running.' He winks. 'And I've worked up quite a sweat.'

'Yeah, but …' I don't want to articulate how uncomfortable the idea of him going in the shower here makes me. 'You don't have a change of clothing.'

'It would still be good to get clean.'

I rack my brain, trying to think of a good reason he shouldn't take a shower. I can't think of anything logical. 'Are you going to use the master bathroom?'

'I was planning to.'

'Doesn't it make you uncomfortable though? I mean, the last person who used that bathroom is a dead woman.'

He shrugs. 'I guess I don't care that much. I mean, that shrink woman disappeared, like, three years ago. It's not like she used the bathroom yesterday.'

It's pregnancy hormones. I'm sure that's what's making me so uncomfortable about this. There's no reason Ethan shouldn't take a shower in the master bathroom. 'Fine. I'm going to stay down here.'

'Sure. Finish your wine.'

Right. That reminds me, I have to pour the rest of my wine down the sink so he thinks I drank it.

It's only when I'm watching Ethan disappear up the spiral staircase that I remember the tape I stashed in the pocket of my coat. When I was in the office, I found that tape recorder, but there were no tapes to play in it. Now I've found the mother lode. Ethan surely wouldn't want me to listen to the tapes, but if he's going to be busy in the shower, I can do what I want.

As soon as the shower starts running upstairs, I retrieve the tape from the pocket of my coat and return to Adrienne Hale's office. The tape recorder is right where I left it—on that beautiful mahogany desk. I sit down in the leather chair and examine the buttons on the dusty tape recorder. Record, Play, Rewind, Fast-Forward, Stop/ Eject, and Pause.

Tentatively, I press the Stop/Eject button. The tape deck pops open.

I blow some of the dust off the tape recorder, then I pick up the tape I found in the hidden room. The initials on it are PL. Next to that, it says #2. And the date is from about six years ago. I remove the tape from the case and shake it out, then slide it into the tape deck. With one quick movement, I push the tape deck closed.

I'm not sure if the batteries in the tape recorder are functional. There's a chance that the eject function is spring loaded or something like that. How long do batteries last if you're not using them? Ethan would probably know the answer to that. But he wouldn't want me listening to these tapes, so I can't ask.

I push my index finger against the Rewind button. Instantly, I hear a whirring noise as the tape goes back to the beginning. Looks like the battery still works.

After about a minute, there's a click, and the rewind process stops. The tape is at the beginning. Ready for me to listen.

My finger hovers over the Play button. Am I really going to do this? Am I really going to listen to the private sessions from Dr Adrienne Hale that she recorded and hid away in a secret closet?

Yes. Apparently, I am.

CHAPTER 10

TRANSCRIPT OF RECORDING

This is session #2 with PL, a twenty-five-year-old female experiencing PTSD after surviving an extremely traumatic incident.

PL: 'Hi, Dr Hale.'
DH: 'You look pale today. Please … sit down.'
PL: 'I'm okay. I just … I haven't been sleeping well.'
DH: 'You mentioned the nightmares during your first visit.'
PL: 'Yes. Like I'm reliving it. Like it's happening all over again.'
DH: 'I know you had a lot of trouble talking about it at your first visit, but if you feel more comfortable with me this time, it would help me so much to hear what happened that night in your own words.'
PL: 'It's so hard to talk about it. It's easier to talk About … other things.'
DH: 'But I'm here to help you. I can't help you if I don't know what you went through.'

PL: 'Yes. Yes, I understand, but ...'

DH: 'Please try. You can take your time. We've got the entire session ahead of us.'

PL: 'It was just ... it was the worst night of my life, Dr Hale. I lost everything.'

DH: 'Just start from the beginning.'

PL: 'Well, I ... I mean *we* ... we rented the cabin for the weekend, and we were so looking forward to it. We were having such a good time, even though it ended up raining all weekend. We hung out, roasted marshmallows in the fireplace ...'

DH: 'And then?'

PL: 'It happened after Cody and I had already gone to sleep. Megan and Alexis had gone off to their own rooms. I was sound asleep ... the fresh air always makes me so tired, and we had a few drinks ... And then I woke up to screaming.'

DH: 'Yes?'

PL: 'It was Cody. He was screaming next to me in bed, and ... and there was blood all over his chest. I woke up, and a man was standing over him, holding a knife. It was hard to see because it was raining out and the sky was so dark. I couldn't make out his face, but I could see his wet hair plastered to his skull. And I could *smell* him. He had that wet dog smell, but also something else. Something rotten.'

DH: 'That sounds terrible.'

PL: 'I wake up sometimes during the night, and I still smell it. I smell it everywhere in my room. That awful, rotten smell ... Oh God ...' [*breaks down crying*]

DH: 'It's okay. It's okay to cry. This is a safe space.'

PL: 'I just … I can't …'

DH: 'Please take a tissue.'

PL: 'It's not fair! Cody and I were supposed to get married next week. We were going on our honeymoon to Bermuda. I was supposed to spend the rest of my life with him, and now … now he's buried in a coffin under the ground. Whenever I think about it …'

DH: 'It's okay. It's going to be okay.'

PL: 'How? *How* is it going to be okay, Dr Hale? The man I was going to marry is *dead*. My two best friends are *dead*. My mother always used to say, if there was a nut job within fifty miles, they would find me. And that night, he found me. I've got a scar on my belly to remember him by forever.'

DH: 'It wasn't your fault though.'

PL: 'It's not fair that they're all gone, and I'm still here. I should be dead to.'

DH: 'Don't say that.'

PL: 'It's true, Dr Hale. That's what the doctor told me at the hospital. I could have died.'

DH: 'But you didn't. You survived. You're a survivor. You could have bled to death in that cabin, but you ran through the rain and mud, and you flagged down a car to help you. That's why you're alive.'

PL: 'I don't feel like a survivor. I feel like … like a mess. I can't sleep. I can't even hold down a job.'

DH: 'That's what you're here for. To get better. This is just the beginning.'

PL: 'If they had caught him, I could move on. But every time I close my eyes, I imagine he's at my window. Watching me sleep.'

DH: 'The key word is "imagine." He's not really there.'

PL: 'You don't know that! After all, I'm the only one who can identify him. I'm sure he wants me dead.'

DH: 'You can't think that way. You're safe now. If he were going to find you, he would've done it already. This is an impulsive man.'

PL: 'I'm going to lose my mind, Dr Hale. It's all I can think about. Every time I get into my car, I feel like he's following me. As I was driving here, I was sure he was in the car behind me.'

DH: 'But you know that's all in your head.'

PL: 'I don't know that. You don't know that. For all you know, he *did* follow me here. Maybe he's waiting outside right now. Maybe the second I open the door to your house, he's going to kill us both.'

DH: 'Do you know how unlikely that is?'

PL: 'I ...'

DH: 'Listen to me. You cannot let this psychopath control your life. You are here to get better. Your family cares about you, and that's why they sent you here.'

PL: 'But I'm not getting better.'

DH: 'This is just the beginning. You're going to get better.'

PL: 'Dr Hale ...'

DH: 'I promise you. You will get better.'

CHAPTER 11

TRICIA

PRESENT DAY

I get about forty minutes into the tape when I realize that I've been down here for too long. Like me, Ethan is notoriously slow in the bathroom, but even he has got to be done showering and dressing by now. Any minute, he's going to come down here looking for me.

I lost track of time. There was something about Dr Adrienne Hale's voice that was simultaneously hypnotic and powerful as she advised the young patient featured in *The Anatomy of Fear*, whose friends and fiancé were murdered by a maniac in a cabin in the woods. When she says, *You will get better*, it's like the voice of God himself saying it. No wonder she was such a respected psychiatrist. No wonder so many people struggling with major trauma came to her for help.

Sure enough, footsteps grow louder on the stairs. I quickly eject the tape and pop it back in the case. I shove the cassette into one of her desk drawers seconds before Ethan pops his head into the office.

'There you are!'

I force a smile. 'Here I am.'

He cocks his head to the side. 'You weren't nosing through her desk drawers, were you, Tricia?'

'No, I wasn't,' I answer truthfully.

I hurry out of the office before he can try to figure out what I was doing. He is standing right outside, his hair still damp from the shower. I notice immediately that he isn't wearing the dress shirt and slacks that he had on when we left the apartment. He's wearing a pair of blue jeans bunched up at the ankles and a Yankees T-shirt.

'Where did those clothes come from?' I ask.

'Oh.' Ethan tugs at the collar of the Yankees shirt. 'I found them in one of the drawers in the bedroom. I hung up my shirt and pants, and I'll put them back on in the morning.'

The T-shirt and jeans didn't belong to Adrienne Hale. They're too big for Ethan even and therefore far too big for the psychiatrist's petite frame. But they were in her drawer, so I'm guessing they belonged to her boyfriend. Luke.

'You might want to change before you go to bed too,' he suggests. 'There are tonnes of sleep clothes in the other drawers.'

What's worse—wearing the clothing of a dead woman or wearing the clothing of the man who killed her?

'That's fine. I'll just sleep in my bra and underwear.'

'Suit yourself. Do you want to come upstairs now?'

I look down at my watch. It's getting late, and with the snow still coming down hard, we have little choice but to spend the night here. The idea of it creeps me out more than I thought it would. But we have to do this.

I can do this.

'Fine,' I say. 'Let's go upstairs.'

I cling to the banister as I follow Ethan up to the second floor like he's leading me to my execution. It's so dark outside the window that even with the lights on, the stairwell and hallways are still dark. Probably if someone changed all the bulbs, it would be a comfortable level of brightness. But we're not going to do that now. We're lucky there's any light here at all.

I continue following Ethan down the hall, but I stop short when he leads me to the master bedroom. 'What are you doing?'

He turns and frowns at me. 'What? What's wrong?'

'I'm not sleeping in that bedroom.'

'Why not?'

'Because that dead psychiatrist slept there!'

His shoulders sag. 'Tricia, stop being silly. The master bedroom is by far the biggest room. This is where we're going to sleep when we're living here.'

Yeah, over my dead body.

'Also,' he adds, 'it's the only bed that's made up. I don't even know where she keeps all the sheets and stuff, but I don't feel like searching for it. I'm tired, and I just want to go to sleep. Aren't you tired?'

A wave of exhaustion comes over me out of nowhere. That's been happening to me more and more lately. In the evening, I'll suddenly feel almost overwhelmed by fatigue. I suppose it's because my body is making an entire other person.

In any case, I agree—I don't feel like searching for a linen closet and making up a bed.

'Fine,' I say. 'We can sleep in the master bedroom.'

When we get inside, the first thing I do is try to lock the door. After that mysterious light I saw glowing on the second floor, I don't think I'll be able to sleep without the door locked. Unfortunately, it isn't that simple.

'What are you doing?' Ethan asks from over in the bed. He has stripped off the blue jeans, but he is still wearing the Yankees T-shirt.

'I want to lock the door.'

'I don't think it locks.'

I whip my head around to glare at him. 'What kind of bedroom doesn't have a lock on the door?'

'I don't know, Tricia.' There is an exasperated note in his voice. 'We're in the middle of nowhere, and she lives alone. Why would she need a lock on her bedroom door when there's already a lock on the front door?'

Because there might be somebody in her house and she needed to keep them out while she called for help? Speaking of calling for help, I haven't seen one landline phone in this whole house. These days, most people use cell phones, but given how terrible the reception is out here, it seems reasonable she might have a landline just for safety reasons. But I haven't seen one.

I back away from the bedroom door, too nervous to take my eyes off it. 'How are we going to get out of here tomorrow?'

Ethan adjusts himself in the bed. 'I'm hoping after the storm passes, our cell phone reception will come back.'

'What if it doesn't?'

'Someone will find us soon.' His voice is brimming with confidence that I wish I shared. 'Judy knows we're here. She might be trying to contact us right now. And of course, your mother will come looking for us if she doesn't hear from you in any twenty-four-hour period.'

'That's not true.'

'Oh, come on. You know it is, Tricia.' He pats the empty side of the bed. 'Your family loves you. There's nothing wrong with that.'

Thankfully, Ethan has not been jealous of my relationship with my parents and sister. We're fairly close, and I do talk to my mother practically every day. Ethan's mother and father both died before we were even dating. It was an accident of some sort, but he doesn't like to talk about it—he clams up at any mention of it. At our tiny wedding, out of the thirty guests who showed up, only five of them were Ethan's—all friends, no family. I had to struggle to pare down my guest list, whereas it seemed like he was struggling to come up with five people.

But there's nothing shameful about wanting only five people at your wedding. Frankly, I would have been happier if my mother didn't have to invite her bitter cousin Debbie or my father's perpetually drunk brother-in-law, Bob.

I flick off the light switch and plop down on the right side of the bed. It's the same side I sleep on in our bed at home. It's weird how we have each picked a side of the bed to sleep on, and neither of us can sleep on the opposite side. We've only been together a little longer than a year, but these habits have already become ingrained.

As Ethan wraps his body around mine, his breaths immediately grow deeper. I don't know how he can seem so relaxed here. Usually, I feel safe and warm wrapped in his arms, but I don't right now. I don't feel safe at all.

CHAPTER 12

It's three in the morning, and I'm wide awake.

At some point, I drifted off. After we went to bed, I was tossing and turning, and Ethan finally went downstairs and got me a glass of water, insisting it would make me feel better. Somehow, it did help, and I drifted off to sleep, but then two hours later, I woke up having to pee.

Ever since I found out I'm pregnant, I've been running to the bathroom every hour on the hour. I thought that wasn't supposed to happen until the end of the pregnancy, but I'm ahead of the curve. Ethan even commented on it a few days ago, but I couldn't tell him why.

I just relieved my bladder twenty minutes ago, but I still can't fall back asleep. I roll my head to look over at Ethan, who is snoring softly next to me. He looks like he's getting an excellent night of sleep in this haunted house. I don't know what's wrong with him.

I climb out of bed, the springs on the mattress groaning slightly but not enough to wake my husband.

I walk over to the picture window across the room and stare outside. The lawn in front of the house is completely covered in snow—at least two feet of it. All the trees are caked in white. We're not going anywhere any time soon in Ethan's BMW. Our best chance of leaving is if cell service returns. I realize sleep is a lost cause so I decide to go down stairs. But it's too cold to go down there in a bra and panties. I rifle through the pile of clothing I took off yesterday, but I'm reluctant to put on jeans and a blouse at three in the morning.

Then I see the robe hanging from the bathroom door. It surely belonged to Dr Adrienne Hale. It's bright red, like the way her hair looked in certain lights. I walk over to feel the material—it's made of fleece. Sensible and warm, for a house that gets buried in snow every winter.

Before I can second-guess myself, I tug the robe off the hook and shove my arms into the holes. It fits me perfectly—Dr Hale must have been about the same size as me. It's just as warm and cozy as it looks, and it's even better when I wrap the belt around my waist and cinch it closed. There's no way I'm not wearing this robe now that I put it on.

It's not like I'm stealing it though. I'm just *borrowing* it. For like an hour—tops.

I start to leave the bedroom in my bare feet, but then I spot the fuzzy red slippers shoved up against the dresser. Well, if I'm borrowing her robe, I may as well take the matching fuzzy slippers.

I shut the bedroom door behind me and make my way slowly and carefully down the spiral staircase to the first floor. I'm not sure exactly what to do down here. My best bet is to find a book to read. That has the best chance of putting me to sleep.

I bypass all the bookcases filled with texts about the workings of the mind and head straight to the one in the back—the one stuffed with novels. Of course, that's the bookcase that also conceals the doctor's secret hiding place. I scan the rows of books for the second time. There are plenty of intriguing titles. There's no shortage of things to read.

But once again, my eyes are drawn to *The Shining*. Even though I know it's not a real book. Or maybe that's *why* I'm drawn to it.

I shouldn't. I really shouldn't.

Almost against my will, my fingers go to the spine of the book. After a split-second hesitation, I pull it out the same way I did before, and once again, I hear that click. The bookcase shifts.

The hidden room is now open.

It's easier the second time, especially knowing that Ethan is sound asleep upstairs and won't walk in on me. I pull the door open and immediately find the cord for the light switch with my hand. The single bulb flickers on, revealing once again the rows and rows of cassette tapes.

Given how well organized this room still is, I have a feeling the police never found it. If they had, it would probably be in disarray. But all the tapes are meticulously arranged. Going back ten years, with the most recent dates about three years ago.

Right before her disappearance.

It occurs to me that if the police had listened to these tapes, they might have discovered clues to help them figure out what happened to her. After all, it seems like she was still making recordings right until when she disappeared. Maybe the very same day.

As I examine the tapes, I figure out she has a labelling system beyond just the initials, session number, and date. She also colour codes them. The first session seems to be labelled with blue ink, then all subsequent ones in black ink, with the final session in red. The pattern repeats over and over again. Except for one.

There's a long row of tapes with the initials EJ on them that has a tape labelled in red—the last session—but then, right after, the tapes resume with a date just a week later. So it seems like Dr Hale had her last session with this EJ person, then started up again almost right after. And there's no final session. The last tape with those initials has black pen on it.

That means she was still seeing this patient at the time of her disappearance.

I pluck the tape with the red marker off the shelf. Perhaps it's a privacy violation for me to listen, but it's not like there are any real names on it. And it's not like I'm going to get any sleep tonight.

CHAPTER 13

TRANSCRIPT OF RECORDING

This is session #137 with EJ, a twenty-nine-year-old man with narcissistic personality disorder. This will be our final session.

EJ: 'Hiya, Doc. How are you doing?'
DH: 'I'm well. How are you?'
EJ: 'I got you a present.'
DH: 'Oh?'
EJ: 'It's a bottle of Rustenberg cabernet sauvignon. It's from South Africa, so it's got eucalyptus notes.'
DH: 'Well, thank you.'
EJ: 'I don't know how much you know about wine pairing, but this is a wine you want to eat with steak or a dish that has a heavy, buttery, creamy sauce. It makes the wine earthier because it neutralizes the tannins.'
DH: 'I appreciate the tip. Please have a seat.'
EJ: 'Yeah, sure, of course. I love this part, you know? Where I get to sit on your couch.'
DH: 'Yes. Listen ...'

EJ: 'It's a nice one too. Real leather. You must make the big bucks, Doc. You probably don't even need me buying you bottles of wine! And you don't even take insurance.'

DH: 'Yes. Actually, that's what I wanted to talk to you about.'

EJ: 'About what? Insurance? I haven't used that. My mom has been paying for all the sessions.'

DH: 'That's the thing. She hasn't. I have explained to you multiple times that she feels you have not made enough progress during these sessions and she doesn't want to pay for them any more, and as you know, I don't take insurance.'

EJ: 'But I disagree. I feel like we *have* made a lot of progress. This really helps me, you know? I like coming here.'

DH: 'Whether or not you have the potential to progress during these sessions, it's reasonable that she doesn't want to continue paying after you have been coming to me for over two years.'

EJ: 'Well, that's dumb.'

DH: 'Regardless, this is her decision. And as I explained to you in our last several sessions, I have not received payment for two months now.'

EJ: 'Oh. I get it. This is about money.'

DH: 'Unfortunately, this is a business. I have bills to pay. And if you're not compensating me for my services—'

EJ: 'But I don't have the money, Doc. You're expensive, you know? Who can afford that? I'm not rich like my parents. All I get is this tiny allowance that barely even covers my rent and car.'

DH: 'We have spoken multiple times about how beneficial it would be if you looked for a job.'

EJ: 'Doc, I'm *trying*, okay? I can't get a job. It's not that easy. I don't have a bunch of fancy degrees like you do.'

DH: 'You're a college graduate.'

EJ: 'Yeah, so what? Everybody's a college graduate. Look, I'll pay you eventually. You have my word. Can't I have a tab?'

DH: 'I'm afraid that wouldn't be fair.'

EJ: 'Fair? Fair to who?'

DH: 'Fair to the people who pay for these sessions.'

EJ: 'That's bullshit, Doc! And it's not like you need the money. I mean, you had that bestselling book. I bet you made a fortune. Look at this place you got here. *You* should pay *me* to hear all my interesting life stories.'

DH: 'That's irrelevant.'

EJ: 'Sure it is. I bet you could write a whole book about my life. You would probably make a million bucks off it. That would pay for my sessions, wouldn't it?'

DH: 'It doesn't work that way.'

EJ: 'So you're just going to cut me off because I can't afford your sessions any more? Goodbye and good luck?'

DH: 'I'm sorry. I have spoken to a colleague of minewho accepts your insurance, and he would be happy to take you on as a patient. I've got his number right here.'

EJ: 'So that's it. You're dumping me.'

DH: 'I'm not "dumping" you. I'm referring you to a colleague. If you're able to pay for my sessions in the future—'

EJ: 'Yeah, I'll bet. My money is good enough for you, but I'm not.'
DH: 'That's not true at all. I just can't—'
EJ: 'I should go to the papers about this. I can just see the news story. Big fancy Harvard-educated psychiatrist cuts off a patient in need because he doesn't have enough money.'
DH: 'I don't think the newspapers would be interested in a story like that. But do what you must.'
EJ: 'This is all an excuse, isn't it? You don't actually care about me.'
DH: 'What are you talking about?'
EJ: 'You're probably thrilled about this. You were just waiting for an opportunity to dump me as a patient.'
DH: 'That's not true.'
EJ: 'Bullshit. You were pretending to care about me this whole time. You never cared though.'
DH: 'I care about you. But I can't provide my services for free.'
EJ: 'You're a real piece of work, Doc. I can't believe you. And after I came here with a *gift* for you.'
DH: 'You can have the wine back if you want it.'
EJ: 'I don't. Keep it.'
DH: 'As I said, I'm sorry.'
EJ: 'Sorry? You don't know what sorry is. You're going to be *really* sorry you kicked me out of here.' [*pause*]
EJ: 'You hear me, Doc?'
DH: 'I'm going to have to ask you to leave now.'
EJ: 'Fine. I'll leave. Now that I know what you're really like, I wouldn't keep coming to you if you begged me. And I bet anything, someday you *will* beg me.'

CHAPTER 14

TRICIA

PRESENT DAY

As the tape ends with a click, I push away a queasy feeling in my stomach.

The man on the tape, EJ, was threatening Dr Hale. Her voice stayed calm through the whole thing, but she had to have been a little shaken. She was just good at hiding it.

Would the police have looked for EJ after Dr Hale disappeared? Maybe not. It's not clear whether she kept a list of her patients. And the newspapers didn't list other suspects besides her boyfriend.

Also, there was something creepy about his voice. I can't put my finger on it. Something creepy and also *familiar*.

It hits me now that he mentioned in the beginning of the tape that he had brought her a bottle of wine. A bottle of cabernet sauvignon from South Africa. When Ethan brought out the wine, he mentioned it was from South Africa. Was it the same bottle of wine? It seems too much of a coincidence that Dr Hale had *two* bottles of cabernet sauvignon from South Africa.

It had to have been the same bottle. She must've never opened the bottle and stashed it away somewhere. I wonder where Ethan even found the bottle. He never told me.

In any case, Dr Hale intended to terminate her sessions with EJ. Yet there are several more tapes with his initials on them made subsequent to this recording. Did he somehow come up with the money to pay? Even if he did, I would have been shocked if she took him back after the way he threatened her.

Yet she took him back. She clearly did. But why?

The only way to know would be to listen to the next tape.

I stand up from Dr Hale's desk, intending to go back to the hidden room and find the next tape in the EJ series. But before I can get out of the room, I hear a crash coming from somewhere nearby.

I freeze and clasp a hand over my mouth. What was *that*? Did Ethan come downstairs? That's got to be what the sound was.

But in my heart, I know it isn't.

We saw a light on upstairs when we were approaching the house. The refrigerator is filled with newly purchased food. And there was a half-drunk glass of water on the kitchen counter. Yes, we checked every room, but I'm still not convinced. This house has a lot of secret places and passages to hide.

Of course, there's one other possibility. Perhaps this house is haunted by the ghost of Adrienne Hale. Maybe her soul is restless because her murderer is still out there. Maybe she's mad that I put on her red robe.

Oh God, pregnancy is making me paranoid.

Much like the bedroom upstairs, there's no lock on the door to the office. That means I can't even barricade myself in the room overnight. And there's no way to contact Ethan and try to wake him up. My only comforting thought is that it seems like whoever is in this house doesn't want to be found.

Then again, maybe they don't want to be found by *Ethan* but would be less bothered about being found by a smaller, less muscular person.

In any case, I'm not spending the night in this office. I rifle through the other drawers in the desk, looking for something I can use as a weapon. The first drawer is mostly filled with papers and the cassette tape I had stuffed inside earlier. The second drawer has more papers and a roll of duct tape. My father always claims there are a million uses for duct tape, but I don't think it can be a weapon—I can't imagine fashioning duct tape into a knife. The third drawer has more office supplies, including a pair of scissors that look pretty sharp. It'll have to do.

Armed with the pair of scissors, I grab the doorknob and twist it. I keep the scissors in my right hand as I yank the door open. I'm ready to confront whoever is out there.

Except the living room outside the door is completely silent.

'Hello?' I call out. No answer.

My hand holding the scissors is shaking. I take a few steps forward, squinting into the mostly dark living room.

I spot a light switch and flip it on, my grip tightening on the scissors.

No. Still nobody.

My breathing slows. I don't see anyone out here. No trace of movement anywhere. The living room is silent and empty. I don't know what that sound was, but it could have come from upstairs. After all, there *is* another person in this house—Ethan.

But then my heart drops into my stomach.

The painting of Dr Adrienne Hale. The one that Ethan took down and placed facing away from us. It's back on the wall. And Dr Hale's green eyes are boring into me.

CHAPTER 15

It takes all my self-restraint to keep from screaming.

I could have accepted that we imagined the light in the window or that it was some optical illusion. I could even have reluctantly accepted that Judy might have purchased some white bread and bologna for the refrigerator. But that portrait …

Ethan took it down. I saw him take it down. It wasn't on the wall when we went to bed. And now it is.

Still gripping the scissors, I race up the spiral stairs so fast that I nearly trip and topple down. Thankfully, I regain my balance and make it the rest of the way to the bedroom. I fling open the door to the master bedroom, where Ethan is still sound asleep.

I close the door behind me, looking around for something to wedge under the doorknob. There's a trunk in the corner of the room that looks sort of heavy. I can shift it over so that it blocks the door. It won't stop anyone from coming in here, but it will slow them down.

Ethan is stirring in the bed from all the noise I'm making. He rubs his eyes. 'Tricia?'

'There's someone downstairs.' I can't keep the panic out of my voice. 'Somebody in the living room.'

Ethan sits up in bed, his eyes suddenly wide open. 'You saw someone down there?'

'Well, no. But I heard a noise.'

He groans. 'Christ, Tricia. All this over a noise? It was probably the house settling.'

'It was not the goddamn house settling! It was a *crash*.' He still doesn't seem perturbed. 'So it was some snow sliding off the roof. I mean, I can think of a million things that could make a noise like that.' He inhales sharply at the sight of the scissors in my hand. 'What the hell are you doing with those?'

'There's an intruder in the house!'

'Yeah, but …' He rubs his eyes again. 'What do you think? That somebody is burglarizing us during a blizzard in the middle of nowhere?'

'Maybe somebody was squatting here. And they're still here in the house somewhere.'

'Maybe …'

Of course, that doesn't explain what I saw downstairs. The painting was moved. Why would a squatter do that? 'The painting was moved,' I finally say. 'That's how I know somebody was down there.'

'That's what you're worried about?' A crease forms between Ethan's eyebrows. '*I* moved the painting.'

'You did?' It didn't even occur to me that he would have put the painting back. I guess we agreed that we would fix anything we moved before we left the house.

I suppose he must've done it when he went down to get me water.

'Tricia, you're freaking me out.' He reaches for me, his hand landing on my shoulder. 'Are you okay?'

Maybe it's the pregnancy making me paranoid. But I can't tell him that. 'I'm fine. I just … I got scared for a minute.'

'Can you please put down the scissors?'

Obligingly, I allow Ethan to pry the scissors out of my hand and put them on the dresser. When the scissors are safely out of the way, he wraps his arms around me. I rest my head on his right shoulder and feel instantly better. I'm lucky that he's so levelheaded. I tend to get worked up easily over things, so he's a good balance for me. I'm really lucky to have him.

'Nobody else is in this house but us.' He laces one of his hands into mine. 'And even if there were, I would protect you.'

'You promise?'

'I promise.' He squeezes my body close to his. 'We're a team now, you and me. We are always there for each other, no matter what. I'm here for you, Tricia, for the rest of our lives. I promise you that. I'll never let anything happen to you.'

My heart rate gradually slows. He's probably right about the crash. There are plenty of things that could've made a loud noise. Hell, it could have been the dishes we precariously stacked in the kitchen. Anything could have done it. We looked everywhere and didn't see another soul in this house.

'I love you,' he says.

'I love you too.'

We lie back down together in the bed, his arms still wrapped around me. It occurs to me that right now is the perfect time to tell him about the baby. It's such a wonderful moment between the two of us. But as I sink deeper into his arms, I feel suddenly exhausted. I don't have the energy to have that conversation with him right now. All I want is to go to sleep.

And the next thing I know, I'm drifting off.

CHAPTER 16

ADRIENNE

BEFORE

I'm running late.

I tap my fingers impatiently on the steering wheel. This is not like me. I pride myself on always being prompt. But I was finishing up the last chapter of my proof copy of *The Anatomy of Fear*, and I just couldn't stop reading. I'm so incredibly proud of that book. It's a conglomeration of the personal accounts of several patients who have survived intense fear-inducing incidents and my expert analysis of those accounts as well as advice to readers who may have experienced something similar.

This book will really help people. It's my crowning achievement.

The light in front of me turns from yellow to red—good God, it will take an eternity to wait for another green light at this intersection. Without thinking about it, I shove my foot onto the gas pedal to breeze through seconds after the light has turned. I hold my breath for a second, bracing myself for the sound of police sirens.

But they don't come.

Technically, I went through a red light. While I don't endorse breaking the law, there are mental-health benefits to doing so. A psychological study demonstrated that cheating or breaking rules results in an unexpectedly good mood afterward. As well as a brief sense of freedom from all rules. So perhaps we should all bend the rules sometimes.

I reach the mall parking lot with one minute to spare until my clinic begins. I don't advertise this fact, but once a week, I volunteer my time at a low-income clinic in the Bronx. I handle medication management for patients with serious psychiatric issues. I'm the only psychiatrist they have at the clinic, and these patients are desperate for my help. Many have been waiting years to see a trained psychiatrist.

The sessions I have at my house are the ones that pay the bills. And while I do have some challenging patients who have been through real trauma, like some of the people in my latest book, the majority of my roster is composed of unfulfilled housewives of rich bankers or lawyers or else their adult children, like EJ, who are going to my sessions on their parents' dime—a desperate attempt to push them out of the nest.

The patients at the free clinic *need* me. I make a real difference here. I even donated a sizable chunk of my book earnings to the clinic when I found out that they were in financial trouble and might shut down.

It's lunchtime and a beautiful day, so the strip mall parking lot is packed with cars. I'm already running late, and my blood pressure escalates as I cruise down three lanes in a row without finding any parking. There is a spillover lot, but it's a ten-minute hike back to the clinic from there. The clinic has booked back-to-back patients, and many of these appointments run over their meager allotted time, so I can't afford to be late.

I finally see a spot at the end of the fourth aisle I check.

Thank God. I'll only be about a minute late.

I roll down the aisle, making a beeline for the spot with my turn signal on. But a split second before I can get there, a red Jetta turns into the aisle, tires squealing. Before I can blink my eyes, the car dives into the empty spot.

I sit there in my Lexus, the turn signal still blinking. Usually, I don't let things bother me. But I've got to get to my clinic. My first patient is a man with schizophrenia who is convinced that he is Superman, and I want to see if the new dose of Geodon will be enough to keep him from making a flying leap off the roof of a building with the presumption that he will soar through the air. I don't have time to spend the next ten minutes searching for parking.

So I do something I shouldn't do. I lay the palm of my hand onto my horn and let it rip.

I know the second the sound rings out that it's absolutely the wrong thing to do. Perhaps if I got out of the car and explained my dilemma, he might have listened. But then again, the driver knew I was waiting for that spot. He knew exactly what he was doing.

A man in his thirties with short hair and a pair of Ray-Bans pushed up the bridge of his nose gets out of his vehicle. I honk again. He grins at me with a mouth full of white teeth and sticks up his middle finger. Then he walks away.

He has a lot of nerve. As he walks right in front of my car, I muse to myself that all I would have to do is switch my foot from the brake to the gas and it would change his entire world. It would wipe that smirk off his face, that's for sure.

But I'm a civilized person. I will not mow down a pedestrian in the middle of a crowded parking lot.

What I'm going to do is calmly find another parking spot.

When I arrive at the clinic, I am huffing and puffing and sincerely regretting my choice of heels. I will certainly have blisters tonight, and after all that, I'm still fifteen minutes late. It's an embarrassment. Not to mention my pink face, my hair coming loose from the French twist I carefully tied, and the beads of sweat on my forehead.

'Dr Hale!' Gloria, the plump, middle-aged receptionist, beams at me when I walk in. 'How are you?'

Those three useless words. How does she think I am?

I'm sweating like a pig. 'Is Mr Harris in the room?'

'Actually, he rescheduled.' She smiles, revealing a gold filling right in front. 'So you have five minutes until your first patient.'

I feel a rush of relief, accompanied by a flash of annoyance that Gloria couldn't have called or texted me to inform me of the cancelled visit. She manages to track down the phone number of every single eligible male in her family between the ages of thirty and fifty, but she can't manage to give me a heads-up about a cancellation.

'Hey, Adrienne. How's it going?'

I swivel my head to the computer station behind the front desk, peering at the man navigating the screen with an ergonomic mouse. When I donated money to the clinic, part of it was earmarked to convert the entire clinic from paper records to electronic medical records. I found the entire paper system maddening, and it allowed things to fall through the cracks, to the detriment of my patients. And this man, Luke Strauss, has been enlisted to help the clinic transition. Technically, he works for the EMR company, but it seems like he has become a fulltime employee at the clinic recently as the technologically illiterate clinicians struggle with the new system. I must admit that I am one of them, although in the end, it will pay off. Electronic medical records are the present—this clinic was living in the past.

'It's been a rough morning,' I admit, because I believe Luke actually wants to know the answer.

'Yeah.' He cocks his head to the side. 'I can see that.

How about some coffee?'

It is not in any way Luke's job to get me coffee, but I know from experience that he will insist on getting it despite my protests. So instead, I nod. 'Thank you.'

He winks at me. 'One cream, no sugar.' He's got it right. Not that I'm surprised.

Gloria follows Luke with her eyes as he darts back to the break room to pour me a cup of cheap coffee. When he's out of sight, she grins at me. 'He's cute, isn't he?'

I shrug because I don't want to encourage her. Is Luke Strauss cute? I suppose some women would think so. Women who like men that walk around in dress shirts badly in need of ironing, poorly knotted ties, dark brown hair that looks like he rolled out of bed five minutes ago, eyeglasses smudged at the edges, and jaws that should have been shaved yesterday. Would it kill him to tuck in his shirt? I rarely date, but when I do, I don't date slobs. The best I can say is he smells of fresh soap. He's a *clean* slob, but a slob nonetheless.

'And he likes you,' Gloria adds.

I pretend not to hear her. I don't want to acknowledge that I am aware Luke likes me. However, I do not wish this relationship to progress past him fetching me coffee and showing me how to send a prescription for Seroquel to the outpatient pharmacy.

Luke returns with my cup of coffee. The liquid is black, and he's brought me a little cup of cream on the side as well as a stirring stick in the cup itself. I didn't even have to tell him that's how I wanted it. Somehow he figured out that I wanted to add the cream myself.

'Thank you,' I say.

The corner of his lips quirks up. 'I hope that helps.'

I pour the container of cream into my coffee. I stir it slowly, until the black morphs into a tan colour. I take a long sip and let out a sigh. 'I needed that.'

'You must be exhausted, Doc,' Gloria remarks. 'You got that big drive both ways. What is it—an hour?'

My fingers dig into my coffee cup. 'Something like that.'

Luke arches an eyebrow. 'You live in Manhattan?'

'No, she doesn't.' Gloria won't let me get a word in edgewise. 'She lives out in Westchester. In a fancy schmancy house. All by herself.'

I silently curse the fact that Gloria is privy to my home address. But I appreciate that Luke didn't know. He may have a pointless and irritating crush on me, but he's not a stalker—I'll give him that much.

'It's not safe out there,' Gloria rambles on. 'All by yourself, in the middle of nowhere. You probably don't even have an alarm system.'

It's an echo of what Paige said to me when she dropped off the proof copy of my book. Why is everyone so convinced I can't take care of myself? 'I'm fine. Really.'

'You know …' Luke looks up at me from the computer. He has long eyelashes for a man. 'A security system isn't a bad idea. I just put one in for my mother. It was easy, and now I feel like she's a lot safer.'

Gloria shoots me a look as if to say, *See? I told you that you need an alarm system. And also, Luke is such a wonderful son to his mother. Don't you want to go out with him?*

I smile thinly. 'I'll think about it.'

I won't think about it. I am perfectly fine the way I am.

CHAPTER 17

TRICIA

PRESENT DAY

I manage to sleep through the entire rest of the night, and according to my watch, it's almost nine o'clock when I wake up the next morning.

Ethan isn't in the bedroom any more, but there's a piece of paper on his side of the bed. It's a note for me. He scribbled in black ink: *Making breakfast downstairs. Didn't want to wake you*.

He's so thoughtful.

I reach for my purse that I left on the nightstand. The first thing I do is grab my phone—still no service. I wonder if Ethan had better luck. I doubt it.

I do a few stretches in the bed, then I force myself to get up. I walk over to the gigantic window near the bed and stare out at our surroundings. Oh my God, there is a *lot* of snow. Everything is covered in a thick blanket of white. Every tree, every bush—the road we took to get here is decimated by snow. I'm sure the BMW is probably just a big lump of white at this point.

We aren't getting out of here soon. That much is certain. I have to make the best of this time. I can't bring myself to take a shower in that bathroom, but I brush my teeth with my finger using what I assume is three-year-old toothpaste. It makes me feel a little better.

My honey-blonde hair is a complete rat's nest after last night. I splash some water on it, then do my best to comb it out using my fingers. There's a hairbrush on one of the shelves in the bathroom, which still has a few dull red strands in it. I'm not touching that hairbrush. My fingers will have to do the trick.

I throw on my jeans and blouse from last night as well as my socks, which are dry but slightly crusty. It does seem a bit of a shame to be wearing my old clothing when there's an entire walk-in closet filled with designer outfits in approximately my size, but I'm not touching any of that stuff. It's too creepy.

When I get down the stairs, I can hear Ethan singing to himself in the kitchen. I pass by the living room and discover he's taken the portrait down again. I'm obscenely grateful that he took it down again so I won't have Dr Hale staring at me. We just have to remember to put it back before we leave.

When I get to the kitchen, Ethan is wearing the Yankees shirt again and the too-long blue jeans. Now that I'm closer, I can make out what song he's singing. 'I'm Walking on Sunshine.' He always likes to sing in the shower or while he's cooking—he actually has a nice singing voice—but he rarely belts it out quite like this. He is in a *really* good mood.

'Hey, Tricia.' He winks at me as he stirs something in the frying pan. 'Sleep okay?'

I nod. 'What are you making?'

'I found some eggs.'

As he says the words, the smell of eggs hits me. All at once, my stomach lurches. I try to suppress it, but I can't. I race over to the kitchen sink and vomit up the residuals of the bologna sandwich I ate last night while Ethan looks on in horror. The vomiting seems to go on for several minutes, followed by another good minute of retching.

I guess this is what morning sickness is like.

'Jesus Christ.' He shuts off the stove. 'Are you all right?'

'Uh-huh.' I run the faucet and scoop up a little water with my hand to rinse out my mouth. I hate vomiting.

Not that anyone *likes* vomiting, but I find it particularly distasteful. 'I'm fine.'

'Was it something you ate?'

'No. I just ...'

'You just what?'

Ethan is staring at me now, his forehead bunched up. He's really worried about me. I could lie and blame it on the bologna sandwich, but I have to tell him eventually. May as well get it over with.

'There's something I need to tell you, Ethan.' His eyes darken. 'Okay ...'

Tell him. Just tell him, you wuss. What's he going to do—fly into a furious rage, murder you, and bury your body in the snow?

'I'm pregnant,' I blurt out.

His mouth falls open. The fork he had been holding clatters to the kitchen table. 'You're ...'

'I'm so sorry. It wasn't intentional, obviously. It just happened, you know? One of those things.' I'm rambling now, but I can't help it. 'I was using my birth control and ... Did you know antibiotics keep birth control from working? I didn't know that. And anyway, so, I just found out. Well, about a week ago. And I know we said we were going to wait two years, but ...'

'Hang on.' He holds up a hand. 'This is for sure? You're definitely pregnant?'

I hang my head. 'Yes. I ... I'm sorry.'

'That's so ...' Ethan is quiet for a second, searching for the right words. I brace myself. 'That's so ... great! That's *fantastic*!'

I take a step back, trying to figure out if I've heard him right. 'What? I thought you wanted to wait.'

'Well ...' He scratches at the back of his neck. 'I thought *you* wanted to wait. Honestly, I wanted to start a family right away, but I didn't want to freak you out. I've already travelled and done all that stuff. But what I really want right now is to have a baby.' He reaches out to take both of my hands in his. 'With you.'

It feels like an enormous boulder has been lifted off my shoulders. 'You mean that? You're not just saying that to make me feel better?'

'No! Why do you think I've been wanting to buy a house? I want to fill it with kids!'

'Oh my God.' I squeeze his hands in mine. 'This is such a relief. I thought you were going to be so angry when you found out.'

He raises an eyebrow. 'When do I ever get angry with you?'

He has a point. He's never angry with me. Annoyed sometimes, but he always seems even-tempered around me. But there was that phone call I overheard with his employee. Where he was screaming at the poor guy. But I can't bring that up.

He chuckles. 'No wonder you've been acting so nutty. It all makes sense now.'

I bristle slightly. I don't think I've been acting *that* nutty. Although I suppose I did barricade the bedroom door at three in the morning.

'I'm going to throw out these eggs.' Ethan lifts the frying pan off the stove. 'They obviously don't agree with you. I'll make you some toast.'

'You don't have to do that.'

He leans over and kisses me on the tip of my nose. 'Will you please let me take care of my pregnant wife?'

'Fine then.' I feel myself smiling. 'Also, thank you for taking the portrait down again. It was really freaking me out.'

'Again?'

'Right.' I watch as he scrapes the partially cooked egg off the frying pan. 'I assume you took it down again this morning.'

Ethan looks at me like I've lost my mind. 'No, I took it down last night. Remember? We were sitting together on the couch, and it was freaking you out, so I took it down.'

'*No.*' My good mood is evaporating. 'You said that you put it back up last night. Like, when you went down for water?'

'I never put it back up. Why would I do that?'

'Because you said you did!' Beads of sweat are sprout ing on my palms. 'At three in the morning, I asked you if you put the painting up again, and you said you did!'

'No. You asked me if I *moved it* last night. And I said I did. I moved it when we were sitting on the couch. I took it down. You *saw* me take it down.'

Oh God. This is *not* what I needed to hear. 'Ethan, last night when I went downstairs, the painting was back up. So if you didn't do it, somebody else did.'

He drops the frying pan in the sink with a clank and turns to look at me. 'I don't understand what you're saying, Tricia. You think somebody came into the living room and put the painting back up? Then later in the night, they took it back down? That's what you think?'

Well, when he says it like that … 'I know it sounds wild.'

'A bit.'

'But I know what I saw.'

'Do you?'

I glare at him. He is seriously losing all the good-husband points he earned a few minutes ago. '*Yes.*'

'I'm just saying …' He folds his muscular arms across his chest. 'It was three in the morning. The house is really dark. You were kind of sleepy and out of it. Is it possible you could be mistaken?'

'No. It's not possible.'

'Are you sure?'

I want to shout at him that I know what I saw. I could never *imagine* those green eyes staring at me. It's not something I could make a mistake about.

But the more times he asks me about it, the more I wonder. It *was* the middle of the night. And the house *is* very dark. Is it possible that I could have *thought* I saw it, like a mirage?

'I guess it's possible,' I mumble.

Ethan seems satisfied with this. But I'm not. Something is going on with this house. I'm sure of it, even though he doesn't believe me.

CHAPTER 18

After breakfast, we regroup at the kitchen table and come up with a plan to get out of here.

Neither of us has cell service, and there are no land lines to be found in the house. Moreover, the storm last night dumped what looks like about ten feet of snow on the area surrounding the house. We can just barely see Ethan's BMW from the window, and it looks like it's just a big mound of snow. He's got a shovel in the trunk, but it won't be enough. Not enough to get out of here anyway.

'I'm hoping a plow will come at some point,' Ethan says. 'I assume Judy would have called one.'

'Yeah.' He looks more optimistic than I feel. 'Maybe.'

'Look, worse comes to worst, we may be stuck here for the day. We've got food and water and electricity. It's not that bad.'

'Yeah …'

He places his palms on the kitchen table and pushes himself to his feet. 'I'm going to head over to the car and get my laptop so I can do some work. Do you want me to get anything for you?'

My stomach sinks. 'You're leaving me here?'

'Just for like fifteen minutes.'

It won't be fifteen minutes. It took us almost fifteen minutes to walk from the car to the house last night in all that snow. 'I want to go with you.'

'Absolutely not. Tricia, you're pregnant. And you have wholly inadequate footwear.'

I suppose he's got a point. It wouldn't be right to make him carry me piggyback to the car and back. Of course, I could borrow a pair of Dr Hale's boots. We do seem to be the same size …

No. I'm not doing that.

'Fine,' I grumble. 'But you promise you'll hurry back?'

'I'll be back before you can say "dream house."'

I am *not* saying 'dream house.'

I clear our plates away while Ethan goes over to the front door, where he left his coat and boots. I watch him shove his feet into his black boots, suppressing the urge to cling to his leg and beg him not to leave me here. Then again, in the light of day, the house isn't nearly as frightening. And when I see the portrait on the floor, facing away from me, it seems impossible that it was up on the wall last night. It seems more like some sort of wild dream. Ethan blows me a kiss from the front door, stuffs his beanie onto his blonde hair, and then he's gone. And I'm all alone.

I take a few slow, deep breaths, trying not to panic. I wish there were a television in this house so I could zone out in front of a screen, but I haven't been able to find one in all my travels. I guess Dr Hale didn't have a television.

What sort of psychopath doesn't own a television in this century?

It only makes me want to learn more about her. And of course, my thoughts immediately go back to the cassette tapes.

Ethan won't make it back from the car for at least half an hour. That will give me time to listen to at least part of a couple more tapes. I'm dying to know what happened in the session after the one I just listened to. Why did she agree to take that man back? Dr Adrienne Hale does not strike me as a pushover.

Before I can second-guess myself, I hurry to the bookcase in the back. I don't even hesitate before I locate *The Shining* and tug on the spine. I hear that now familiar click and I slip inside the room, grabbing the cord to turn on the light.

This time, I decide to swipe a bunch of the tapes. I can stash them in one of the drawers in the office. I take all the EJ ones recorded after the tape marked in red. Then I take a selection of other tapes from around the same date. It must've been right before Dr Hale disappeared, because there's nothing recorded later than that.

I'm going to hear the information that the police missed. I'll listen to everything that happened to Dr Hale in the months leading to her disappearance. The mystery that the entire country was talking about for almost a year. I scan the shelves one more time. That's when the one tape labelled differently catches my eye once again. LUKE. The boyfriend. The one the police thought killed her. Why does she have a recording of him? Was he her patient? But if he was, why is his tape labelled differently than all the others?

My mother always said I'm too curious for my own good.

I grab the LUKE tape and add it to the pile. I'll have time to listen to at least one of these tapes before Ethan gets back.

I close the door to the hidden room and carry my stack of tapes to Dr Hale's office. I stash them in the bottom drawer of her desk, where I found the scissors last night. I select one of them at random and pop it into the tape recorder.

My finger hesitates over the Play button. I desperately want to listen to these tapes, but there's one thing I need to do first.

I get up and close the door to the office. Okay, now I can listen.

CHAPTER 19

TRANSCRIPT OF RECORDING

This is session #89 with GW, a sixty-eight-year-old widow experiencing paranoid delusions.

GW: 'Hello, Dr Hale.'
DH: 'Please have a seat, Gail.'
GW: 'Oh. Yes. Of course. I'm sorry.'
DH: 'Don't apologize. I want you to be comfortable when we're talking.'
GW: 'Yes. I know. I just … I feel like …'
DH: 'Are you okay? You seem especially anxious today. Your hands are shaking.'
GW: 'I just …'
DH: 'Are you taking the medications I prescribed?'
GW: 'No. I'm afraid not.'
DH: 'How come?'
GW: 'Well, I … I know you're going to tell me I'm being paranoid if I tell you this.'
DH: 'Tell me.'
GW: 'I … I think my pharmacist is trying to kill me.'

DH: 'Gail …'
GW: 'I know. You think I'm crazy. You think I'm paranoid. But this time, it's true. I mean, he's a pharmacist. It would be so easy for him to do it. He could just swap out my pills for something else.'
DH: 'Why would you think he wants to kill you?'
GW: 'It's the way he looks at me. I can't describe it. And after he handed me the bag with my pills in it, he winked at me.'
DH: 'So …?'
GW: 'Don't you see, Dr Hale? He was winking at me because he knew there was something bad in the pill bottles.'
DH: 'Maybe he was just being friendly? Or even flirting?'
GW: 'No. Definitely not.'
DH: 'Why would he want to kill you?'
GW: 'Who knows? Because he's a psychopath. You know, people are walking around out there who are just crazy. They don't need a reason to kill you. They just do it because they're crazy!'
DH: 'Gail, I need you to take your medications.'
GW: 'But I can't! Don't you see what I'm saying? If I take those pills, I'm going to die!'
DH: 'Do you remember when you thought the mailman was trying to kill you?'
GW: 'Um …'
DH: 'Gail? Was he actually trying to kill you?'
GW: 'I'm still not sure. I mean, it's *possible*. He was always outside my house at the same time. Right outside my door. Peeking in.'

DH: 'He was delivering your mail, Gail.'

GW: 'There was something funny about it.'

DH: 'The mailman was not trying to kill you. And your pharmacist is not trying to kill you. You really need to take the medications that I prescribed.'

GW: 'That's what my son says too.'

DH: 'So there you go. You should listen to him.'

GW: 'But think about it, Dr Hale. If I were to die, my son would get a big insurance payoff. So he doesn't mind if the pharmacist kills me.'

DH: 'Gail, listen. You have to try to recognize that This … this …' [*pause*]

GW: 'Yes?'

DH: 'Hold on. I just … My phone buzzed. I have to make sure it's not an emergency with one of my patients. It's …'

GW: 'Dr Hale?'

DH: 'Hang on.'

GW: 'Dr Hale? Is everything okay? What does your text message say?'

DH: 'I'm sorry, Gail. I'm afraid we're going to have to reschedule our appointment. An emergency has come up.'

CHAPTER 20

ADRIENNE

BEFORE

I stare at the screen of my phone. It was horribly unprofessional of me to tell Gail to leave right in the middle of a session. But I didn't have a choice. I read the words on the screen for the fifth time:

> Hi, Doc. I have a little video I took of you from a parking lot in the Bronx. I thought you might enjoy watching it!

The message came from EJ. I didn't delete his number from my phone after I terminated him as a patient. I wish I had, but it doesn't matter. I have a feeling he would have found a way to get me this message.

Below the message is a link to a video. I haven't watched it yet. The image on the screen is of me, frozen in time, dressed in the white blouse and gray skirt suit I wore to the free clinic the other day. My hair is whisked behind my head, although it had come partially loose during my hike from my parking spot to the clinic.

I remember that moment in time. And I remember what happens next.

I can't bring myself to watch it. But I must.

I take a deep breath and tap my finger on the video to start it. Immediately, the image of myself unfreezes. The camera follows me for a couple of seconds, then zooms in as I pause in front of a red Jetta.

That asshole who took my parking spot.

The quality of the video is excellent. Naturally, EJ would have the most expensive phone money could buy. You can see the license plate of the car in perfect detail. You can see me fumble around in my purse for something. Then you can see me bend down beside the back tire of the Jetta and look both ways to make sure nobody is watching me. For a split second, the camera catches the glint of a knife in the sunlight just before it sinks into the tire.

Yes. I slashed that man's back tire.

It sounds worse than it is. I was late to a clinic where my patients' lives depend on me. The parking spot was *mine*. I was signaling to take it. He stole it from me, so he committed the crime first. I was simply retaliating.

And yes, I carry a knife in my purse. Sometimes the clinic lets out late, and it's not the best neighbuorhood. I suppose I could carry a can of Mace. I choose to carry a knife.

Slashing that tire was the wrong thing to do. I should not have allowed my anger at that man's rude and selfish behaviour to get the best of me. I should have taken the high road.

And I had no idea anyone was watching me.

I jump in my chair as another text message appears on my phone. The message comes from the same number:

I can see the headline now. Bestselling Author–Psychiatrist Slashes Tires in Parking Lot.

I swallow. He is not wrong that this will make a compelling headline. One that has the potential to destroy me. And it's all on video.

My hands are trembling as I type a reply. It takes me three tries to get it right:

What do you want?

His reply comes almost instantly:

I'm outside your front door.

An icy sensation slides down my spine. I always laughed at people like Paige and Gloria when they suggested I needed a home security system. I always felt safe here. But when I stare down at the words on my phone, I no longer feel safe. I'm not sure I ever will again.

I'm outside your front door.

I glance behind me at the window—the sun dropped in the sky over the last hour, and it's now dark outside. I stand up abruptly from my leather chair, so quickly that it glides across the room, slamming into the wall behind me. I can't ignore these messages. I've known EJ for a long time, and he will not let this go.

I take my phone with me to the front door, clutching it in my left hand much the way Paige did when she came to visit. I consider calling 911 but quickly rule it out.

EJ has done nothing wrong. Yes, he is on my property, but I have no evidence that I terminated him as a patient. He has not breached my front door. And if he shows the police that video of me, my career is over.

He is calling the shots.

My front door is constructed from the same deep-brown wood as the desk in my office—mahogany, I believe—broken up by two opaque panes of glass. There's a lock and dead bolt on the door, but only a few feet away, there's a window that could be easily shattered with a rock. I pass the window on the way and I can make out the shadow in front of my door. I stand there for a moment, hesitating until my phone vibrates in my hand.

> Why are you just standing there, Doc? Open the door for me.

I grit my teeth. I twist open the dead bolt, then turn the lock. I take a quick calming breath, remembering that I know EJ better than he knows me. I know all his strengths and weaknesses. He's intelligent and manipulative, but he's also impulsive. He may have caught me in a moment of weakness, but I can outsmart him.

I yank open the door, and there he is. Wearing a Michael Kors jacket, no doubt purchased with his wealthy parents' money. His sun-streaked blonde hair is slightly disheveled, and he has a smirk on his lips. EJ is handsome—that is undeniable, although he's on the shorter side, which gives him a bit of a Napoleon complex. During the time I have been treating him, he has been in relationships of varying length—anywhere from one night to six months—with countless women.

The one-night stands got off easy. I pity any woman whose path crossed with this man.

'Aren't you going to invite me in, Doc?' he asks.

I don't want him in my house, but again, I have little choice in the matter. So I step back and allow him to saunter inside.

'You got such a nice place here, Doc,' EJ comments like he's seeing it for the first time. 'Nice furniture too. You have great taste. Is that real leather?'

'What do you want?' I say through my teeth.

He takes a step back, blinking at me. 'Hey. Doc, come on. Don't be upset at me.'

'Don't be upset at you?' My right hand balls into a fist while my left still clutches my phone. 'You were following me. You recorded me without my consent.'

'I wasn't following you. It was a coincidence.'

Like many people, EJ has a tell. I know when he's lying. A little muscle under his right eye twitches whenever he tells a lie. It's twitching now, but it's not like I wouldn't know he was lying. How could he possibly just *happen* to run into me at a strip mall an hour away from here?

But it doesn't matter. Whether or not he was following me, he has the video.

I hug my chest. 'What do you want?'

'Look.' EJ focuses his gray eyes on me. 'I don't want to make trouble for you, Doc. I swear. I just felt like you were really helping me, and I was sad when you gave up on me. All I want is to start our sessions again.'

My jaw falls open. 'You want to start sessions again? With *me*?'

'That's right.'

The thought of being alone in the therapy room with EJ makes my skin crawl. 'I don't think that's appropriate. Let me refer you to one of my colleagues. I … I can pay the bill for your sessions.'

There are a few psychiatrists from my training that I would *love* to foist this guy off on. It would be my pleasure. But EJ shakes his head. 'No, you already offered that, and it's not what I want. You and I were making great progress. You're the best. I want *you*.'

'I really feel like I've gone as far as I can with you.'

'I disagree.'

I bite the inside of my cheek. The metallic taste of blood fills my mouth. 'Fine. Two sessions a month.'

'We were doing once a week before.'

'I don't have that many openings in my schedule any more.'

He clucks his tongue. 'I don't know, Doc. Maybe you should *make* an opening then.'

I can do this. I can sit with this man for an hour once a week and pretend to listen to his problems. I've done worse.

'Fine,' I say. 'But that's it, okay?'

EJ holds up his hands. 'That's all I want. Just an hour of your time once a week so I can get better. I won't ask for anything else. I promise.'

As he says the words, the muscle under his right eye twitches.

CHAPTER 21

TRANSCRIPT OF RECORDING

This is session #138 with EJ, a twenty-nine-year-old man with narcissistic personality disorder.

EJ: 'It's nice to be back on your sofa, Doc.'
DH: 'Uh-huh.'
EJ: 'I appreciate you taking me back.'
DH: 'Well, it's not like I had a choice, did I?'
EJ: 'Don't be like that, Doc. Look, you should be flattered. You were really helping me. That's all I wanted. You're so good at what you do.'
DH: 'Yes, well ... what did you want to discuss today?'
EJ: 'I don't know. Lately, I've been feeling bored with everything. Like, there isn't anything exciting going on in my life.'
DH: 'Maybe that's a sign you should look for work.'
EJ: 'I guess. But it seems like it's pointless. Eventually, my parents will die and leave me all their money. So why bother looking for work when I'm going to be rich either way?'

DH: 'Don't you want to earn your own money and contribute to society?'

EJ: 'Not really.'

DH: 'You told me you thought about becoming a sommelier, didn't you? You love wine.'

EJ: 'Yeah, I thought about it. But I started looking into the training, and it's a lot of work, you know? It takes *years* to get a degree.'

DH: 'Something else then. Don't you want your own money? Do you want to rely on your parents for everything until they're gone?'

EJ: 'Well, they're pretty old.' [*pause*] 'And my mother is a terrible driver. One of these days, she'll probably be driving with my father in the car, and she'll just drive right into a Mack truck and they'll both be killed.'

DH: 'You think your mother would drive into a truck? She's that poor of a driver?'

EJ: 'Well, maybe she wouldn't. Maybe the brakes would fail.'

DH: 'I see.'

EJ: 'What's wrong, Doc? You look pale.'

DH: 'You're telling me you would tamper with your parents' brakes …'

EJ: 'No! Hey, come on. I wouldn't do that, Doc. I love my parents, even if they're a pain in the ass. I'm just saying. It could happen. Brakes fail.'

DH: 'I … I'm not sure what to say.'

EJ: 'Anyway, I got a plan to make some money this weekend.'

DH: 'And what's that?'

EJ: 'I'm driving down to the Foxwoods Casino and spending the weekend there.'

DH: 'I'm not sure if that would be considered a reliable plan to make money.'

EJ: 'Aw, I always clean up at the poker tables. I'm really good at it. Trust me. I'll pull in a few Gs on Saturday afternoon, then Saturday night, I'll have some fun.'

DH: 'Fun?'

EJ: 'You know. I'll find a girl.'

DH: 'I see.'

EJ: 'Unless you want to come with me, Doc? I'd love to have you. You're a beautiful woman.'

DH: 'I don't think so.'

EJ: 'Maybe another time.'

DH: 'I don't think so.'

EJ: 'Hey, you want to hear my fantasy?'

DH: 'I've heard your fantasies. I don't think this is productive. We're supposed to be talking about getting your life on track.'

EJ: 'Yeah, but this is *my* therapy session. I *earned* it. And this is what I want to talk about.'

DH: 'You said the reason you want these sessions is that you want me to help you.'

EJ: 'Right, but I've been coming to you for a long time, and we all agree you haven't helped me that much. Maybe it's better to do things my way. Talk about what I want to talk about for a change.'

DH: 'Look—'

EJ: 'And this is what *I* want to talk about. You get me, Doc?'

DH: '…'

EJ: 'Doc?'

DH: 'Fine. Go ahead. Tell me your "fantasy."'

EJ: 'Don't get so worried. It's nothing too wild. I just have this fantasy that I'm sitting at the craps table at Foxwoods, and this insanely hot woman sits down next to me.'

DH: 'Okay …'

EJ: 'She doesn't say one word, doesn't even tell me her name. She just slides a drink in my direction, and that's how I know she wants me. And then she comes up to my room and we go at it all night long, like animals. And when it's over, she leaves and I never see her ever again.'

DH: 'That's beautiful.'

EJ: 'Sarcasm doesn't suit you, Doc. I'm pouring out my heart to you. You could show a little, you know, empathy. Don't they teach you that in shrink school?'

DH: 'I simply don't think these sessions are productive. As I said, I would be happy to refer you to one of my excellent colleagues. I would cover the cost of the sessions.'

EJ: 'No. We're not going to do that.'

DH: 'Why not?'

EJ: 'Because I want *you*.'

CHAPTER 22

TRICIA

PRESENT DAY

The recording comes to a stop, and the tape recorder clicks, turning off automatically. Based on this recording, it sounds like EJ was forcing Dr Hale to continue doing therapy sessions with him. Maybe he was blackmailing her.

Except what was he using to blackmail her?

I'm not sure I can listen to any more EJ sessions. There's something about the sound of his voice that makes my skin crawl. You can tell just from listening to him that he's not a good person.

He's evil. 'Tricia?'

I nearly jump out of my skin at the sound of rapping on the door to the office. I just barely have time to shove the tape recorder into the top drawer of the desk before the door swings open. It's driving me wild that this house doesn't have any locks.

'Tricia?' Ethan is standing at the door, the bottom of his jeans slightly damp from the snow even though he was wearing boots. 'What are you doing in here?'

I pick up a pen that was lying on the desk and tap it purposefully against the shiny wooden surface. 'I decided, since there isn't much to do, I would work on my résumé a little.'

It's a plausible enough lie. At the moment, I'm between jobs. I used to work at an online magazine. You know the kind—twelve tips to make your boyfriend sizzle, five recipes that will get things going in the bedroom, how to drop fifteen pounds without even trying. I was the master at creating clickbait. But then the magazine unexpectedly went belly up right before the wedding. It wasn't like I was going to look for jobs on my honeymoon, so it gave me an excuse to procrastinate. And somehow now it's been almost six months that I've been unemployed.

It's not that I don't want to work. I do. I would love to be a productive member of society. But I remember how long it took to find a permanent position at the magazine, and I'm not excited to start pounding the pavement again. Rejection hurts, even though it's a part of the jobapplication process.

And now house hunting has become yet another excuse to avoid it. After all, moving and possibly renovating a house will be a full-time job. And of course, now my pregnancy.

Ethan is apparently thinking the same thing, because he crinkles his nose. 'You're looking for a job *now*? But we're going to have a baby soon.'

'Not that soon,' I point out, even though I secretly agree with him. 'I don't know if I'll take anything, but it can't hurt to look, right?'

'Right. I mean, you can look if you want. But if you want to stay home during your pregnancy, I'd be okay with that.' He grins at me. 'More than okay.'

I get a warm fuzzy feeling all over my body. I hit the husband jackpot. I don't know why my friends don't like him. Whenever we talk about him, they always say, *This is a red flag*, or *That's a red flag*. But Ethan is a genuinely good guy. What does it matter that he hasn't had many girlfriends before me? And why should the fact that he lost his parents and doesn't have much family be a reason I should avoid him?

My mother would say they're jealous. After all, I have a gorgeous, wealthy husband who just wants me all to himself.

I clear my throat. 'Did you get the laptop?'

He holds his MacBook up triumphantly. 'I almost sunk into about six feet of snow, but I got it.'

I look around the room. When we first came in here, Ethan's eyes lit up and he had talked about how much he wanted to make this room into his office. 'Do you want to work in this room?'

'Actually,' he says, 'not really. It's a big room, and the furniture is nice, but there's no natural light in here. There's just that one tiny window.'

I glance over my shoulder at the window in question. He's right. Most of the rooms have these huge picture windows, but this room doesn't. Maybe that's why she chose it to be the room where she saw patients. Because it's so isolated.

'So I'm going to go work upstairs,' he says. 'You can stay down here if you'd like.'

'Maybe I will.'

'And it's great that you're working on your résumé,' he adds, 'but for the record, I'll happily support you for the rest of your life if that's what you want.'

It's not what I want, but my cheeks flush with pleasure at the offer. He means it—I know that much. He wants to spend his life taking care of me.

Of course, my friends would probably call it yet another red flag. *He's trying to control you with money.* Bullshit. He's just a good guy.

'Anyway,' Ethan says, 'are you all right down here? Is there anything you need?'

'No, I'm fine.'

'Are you sure?'

'I'm sure. Really.'

Now my cheeks are hot because I feel bad that I want him to leave. I want him to go away so I can continue listening to these tapes. It's quickly become a bit of an addiction.

Will the contents of these tapes reveal the secret of what really happened to Dr Adrienne Hale?

I can't leave this house without finding out.

I open the bottom drawer of the desk. I rifle through the cassette tapes inside, and the one that's different catches my eye. LUKE. The boyfriend. Why does she have a recording of her boyfriend?

I pull the tape out of the drawer and remove it from the cover. I eject the session with EJ, and I put the new tape inside the player. Then I press Play

CHAPTER 23

ADRIENNE

BEFORE

'Is Luke here today?'

Gloria's eyes light up at my question. But she has no idea why I want to talk to Luke, and I have no intention of telling her. 'Yes, he's here. He's helping Dr Griffith out in the documentation room in the back.'

My first patient at the free clinic is scheduled in fifteen minutes. I came early today so I could talk to Luke. I wasn't certain if he would be here, but I've noticed he's found an excuse to show up whenever I'm scheduled to work. Coincidence? Perhaps. We'll see.

'Also,' Gloria adds, 'you got another card. And some chocolate.'

She slips me a small box of cheap drugstore mixed chocolates with a little rectangular pink envelope on top. 'Dr Hale' is scrawled on the envelope in ballpoint pen. Even though I'm desperate to find Luke, I take a second to rip open the envelope. I slide out a small card with a lone bird pictured, flying through a blue cloudless sky. I open the card and read the shaky script:

Dear Dr Hale,

I can't tell you how much your help meant to me. When I saw you, I was going through a dark time in my life. If not for you, I'm not sure I would be here any more. You saved my life. Bless you.

Lola Hernandez

I slide the card back into the envelope and slip it into my jacket pocket. This is one I will save. I have a collection, and sometimes I read through them on my own dark days. But there's no time today to dwell on it and pat myself on the back. I have to save my career.

'Don't forget the chocolate, Dr Hale,' Gloria speaks up. The card was thoughtful, but the chocolates are undoubtedly of poor quality. I shake my head. 'You can have them, Gloria. Give them to your grandchildren.'

'You should eat them. Put some meat on your bones. Men like that.'

I flinch. Gloria isn't the first person to comment on multiple occasions that she feels I'm too bony. *Like a skeleton*. I can't imagine how anyone could possibly think my body habitus is any of their business. I don't even dignify her comment with a response. Instead, I turn on my heels and head down the hallway to the documentation room, leaving the box of chocolates behind.

When I'm about ten feet away from the room, I can hear Luke and the elderly Dr Griffith speaking together. Dr Griffith sounds frazzled, which isn't out of the ordinary for him.

'So I just want to look at the note. But every time I click on it, it opens the note for editing or tries to add an addendum.'

'That's because you're double-clicking on the note.

You just want to click on it once to view it.'

'I *am* clicking on it once. See—look what it did.'

'Right. That's because you double-clicked.'

'No, I didn't.'

I enter the documentation room just in time to hear Luke patiently explaining to Dr Griffith the difference between single-clicking and double-clicking for what I'm sure is the third or fourth time. I can tell by the way Dr Griffith's bushy white eyebrows knit together that he doesn't get it. He will *never* get it.

I rap my fist gently against the door. Luke's brown eyes light up when he sees me. Today I have worn a red dress that I located in the back of my closet. Psychological studies have demonstrated that men have more amorous feelings toward women wearing red than any other colour. They are more likely to express the desire to take a woman wearing red out on a date and are also willing to spend more money on the date. Moreover, the men in these studies could not identify the origin of these feelings. They just liked the girl in red.

'Adrienne!' Luke says happily. 'What's going on?'

'Do you have a minute, Luke?'

He looks between me and Dr Griffith, obviously torn between his promise to help the elderly doctor figure out how to click on a note and wanting to help me. Thankfully, Dr Griffith takes pity on him and rises unsteadily to his feet.

'No worries, Luke,' Dr Griffith says. 'We can try to figure it out later.'

Luke rises from his seat to face me as Dr Griffith leaves the room. He looks different today. His sky-blue dress shirt has been ironed, and he's wearing a brown tie, although the knot could be a little tighter. And he's shaved this morning. Usually, he smells like soap, which is not at all unpleasant, but today I detect a different, musky scent. Cologne or aftershave.

'What's up?' he asks.

I wring my hands together. 'I need your help with something.'

His lips curl. 'Fair warning—if you need me to teach you the difference between double-clicking and single-clicking, I'm going to lose it.'

My laugh sounds forced to my own ears. I tried my best to look put together this morning, even though it was difficult because my sleep has been terrible ever since that video appeared on my phone. It took three layers of makeup to cover the purple circles under my eyes. 'No, it's something else. I … I was hoping you could help me install a home security system.'

He blinks his brown eyes behind his glasses. 'What?'

'You mentioned you did it for your mother.' I clear my throat. 'So I thought you could help me out.'

He rubs his thumb along his clean-shaven jaw. 'Right, but—'

'I'd pay you, of course.'

That's the wrong thing to say. His face drops. 'It's not that. I don't need you to pay me. I just think ... You've got that big house and you're probably better off hiring a company to do it for you. I mean, I put something together for my mother but she's just got a tiny little cottage.'

I cringe at the idea of a bunch of strangers on my property, installing cameras and equipment so that they can spy on me. I don't want this equipment so that they can watch me. *I* want to be the one watching.

'I've already bought the equipment,' I say. 'I just need somebody to help me install it. I don't know how to do it myself.'

'It's just that whatever you bought will never be as good as what a professional would install.'

'I don't want a professional.' I dig my nails into the palm of my hand. 'I want you to do it for me. Please.'

'Adrienne—'

'I'll treat you to dinner. Anywhere you want.'

'But—'

'*Please*, Luke.'

His shoulders sag. 'Okay, fine. I'll do it.'

It feels like a weight has been lifted. Having a security system won't protect me from EJ, but I feel better about it. I don't like the idea of him lurking outside my property and following me. I want to know what's going on. I'm not used to this feeling of a lack of control, and I don't like it. 'Thank you, Luke.' Before I can stop myself, I reach out and touch his arm. I'm not a touchy-feely sort of person, but I feel a rush of gratitude toward this man. 'I really appreciate it.'

'No problem.' He smiles at me. He looks different with the ironed shirt and tie and with his face clean-shaven. He's unexpectedly handsome. 'And you don't have to treat me to dinner.'

'I want to.'

'Well, why don't you think about it?'

I consider protesting again, but there's something firm in Luke's voice. I appreciate that he doesn't want to go out to dinner with me unless I want to do it. He's not going to bulldoze me into anything. 'Fine then.'

'So …' He rubs his hands together. 'When do you want to do this?'

'As soon as possible.'

He arches an eyebrow. 'I'm free tonight.' Somehow I knew he would be.

Luke parks his blue Toyota right behind my Lexus, in front of the house. He had my address plugged into his GPS, but I told him that the signal would likely give out after we turned off the main road, so he was better off following me. I usually give my patients specific directions on getting to my house.

'Jesus, Adrienne.' Luke is tugging on his tie to loosen it as he gets out of the Toyota. 'You're really isolated out here. This is the only house for miles.'

It's actually 1.9 miles from the last house we passed. But I decide not to point that out. 'Yes.'

He glances around at the trees surrounding the narrow, unpaved road to my house. 'What do you do when it snows hard? You must get trapped here.'

'I have an arrangement with a plowing company. They plow the entire road for me.'

I brace myself for more questions, but they don't come. Instead, he pops open his trunk and pulls out a box of tools, then follows me to the front door. When I open the door and Luke steps onto the threshold, he lets out a low whistle.

'Wow,' he comments. 'I know.'

'This place is *huge*.'

'Yes, I *know*.'

Luke flashes me a sheepish grin. 'Sorry, I've just never known anyone who lived in a castle before.'

I ignore his comment comparing my home to a castle. 'So I've got the kit I bought to set up the security system over there.' I nod at the cardboard box pushed against the wall. It arrived yesterday, and I spent twenty minutes looking through the instructions and verifying that there was no way on earth that I could set it up on my own.

He chews at the corner of his lip. 'You sure you want me doing this? A professional would—'

'Luke.'

He lets out a long sigh. 'Okay. I'll do it.'

He crouches down to rummage through the cardboard box. I shuffle between my feet, concerned that this job could be too big for him. From my perspective, he's a genius with electronics. But my standards aren't exactly high. The vast majority of employees at the Apple store fall into that category. Still, I'm heartened that he carries around a toolbox in his trunk.

'Do you think you'll be able to do it?' I ask. 'I can't see why not.'

My shoulders relax slightly. 'And can you install the camera to overlook the front door? So I could see who's there from my phone?'

'Sure.'

'Great. Perfect.'

He pulls out a small plastic bag of screws and squints at them through his glasses. 'Do you have any objections to me putting a couple of tiny holes in your wall?'

'Do what you need to do.'

He glances up at me. 'Don't feel like you have to stand there watching me. This won't be quick. Why don't you do some work or something, and I'll let you know when I'm done?'

Truthfully, I would not have minded watching him. I find this sort of thing fascinating. And while I hate to admit it, I'm finding Luke more attractive as I watch him rummaging through his toolkit. As a rule, I don't date. I rarely find a man who seems worth the effort. I always felt like I was immune to the urges most women have.

But as I watch Luke, I wonder if that's true.

I cough, pushing away unwelcome thoughts. 'I'll be working over there, in the room where I see patients. Let me know if you need anything.'

'Will do.'

I spend the next ninety minutes answering emails in my office. I'm dying to go out there and check up on how Luke is faring with the setup, but I don't want to hover over him. So I wait patiently for him to come to me. With every minute, my guilt escalates at how long he's spending helping me.

Finally, when I'm contemplating getting up to check on him, a fist raps on the door to my office. 'Adrienne?'

'Just a moment!'

I quickly finish up the email I'm working on, then get back on my feet. When I come out of my office, Luke is near the door, standing by my bookcase. He's holding one of my books, and it takes me a second to realize it's my newest one—soon to hit bookstores all over the nation.

The Anatomy of Fear.

'Oh, hey.' His cheeks colour. 'Sorry, didn't mean to snoop. I saw the book with your name on it, and I got curious.'

'It's just a proof copy.'

'It looks really interesting.' Again, that sheepish smile. 'I read your other one. It was great. Intelligent but down-to-earth. The sort of thing that would appeal to anyone.'

'Thank you.'

'You probably hear that all the time though.'

'Not that much.' I look down at the copy in his hands. 'This one is coming out in a few months. I'm really proud of it.'

'It's about ... fear?'

I nod, eager to talk about it. When the book releases, there will be book tours and interviews and perhaps television appearances. But as of now, there's been nothing. And I'm dying to talk about my book. 'Basically, it's about people who have survived terrifying situations and how they have coped in the aftermath.'

'Heavy stuff.'

'The most striking case study is a patient, PL, who I've been seeing for a few years now,' I say. 'She was staying at a cabin for the weekend with her fiancé and two of her best friends. Out in the wilderness, no cell phone service, yada yada yada.'

He smiles crookedly. 'Oh, you mean like here?'

'*Nothing* like here.' I shoot him a look. 'Anyway, they were drinking quite a lot and smoking pot, so their guard was down when a man with a butcher knife burst into the cabin.' I lick my lips, recalling the description I wrote in the book.

'He slashed their tires so they couldn't get away. Then he stabbed all four of them, leaving them for dead. My patient survived by pretending to be unconscious. After the assailant left the cabin, she stumbled through the woods until she came across the main road and flagged down a car for help.'

'Jesus,' Luke breathes. 'That's … awful.'

I pull the book out of his hands, flipping through the pages of my own words recounting the story my patient told me of the horrors she had endured. 'The worst part is they never caught the guy who did it. He's still out there somewhere.'

'Oh, wow.' He shakes his head. 'They never found him? Do they know why he did it?'

'Does anyone know why somebody would try to murder four random people in the woods?'

Luke doesn't have an answer for that.

'For a year, she woke up screaming every night.' I can still picture that girl's bloodshot eyes with the dark circles underneath. 'She had nightmares about the man being outside her window. It tortured her that he was still out there. It took a lot of counseling to get her better. Counseling and time.'

'I'm sure your help was a large part of that.'

'I'd like to think I helped her. It's hard to get over that kind of trauma.'

'On that note …' He jerks his head in the direction of the living room. 'Let me introduce you to your new security system.'

For the next half hour, Luke shows me all the hard work he put in to secure my home. There are sensors mounted on all the first floor windows. The control panel is right inside the front door, and he turns away to allow me to punch in my six-digit passcode. It's my late mother's birthday.

'You can arm or disarm your security system once you punch in the code,' he explains. 'This control panel will even allow you to set up a schedule to disarm it at certain times of day if that's what you want.'

'What about the camera?'

'I mounted it outside your front door. I just need to link the feed to your phone.' He holds out his hand. 'If you give me your phone, I'll set it all up for you.'

I left my phone back in my office, so I lead him over there. As soon as he gets my phone in his hands, he quickly installs the app I need and links it to the camera. When he hands it back to me, I can see the image on the screen of the area outside my front door.

'This is incredible,' I breathe. 'Thank you so much.' But Luke doesn't answer me. He's staring straight ahead, at the bookcase in my office. His eyes are locked on a gap between two books. 'What's *that*?'

In all my years of interviewing patients in this office, he is the first person to notice the tape recorder concealed between those two hardcover books. I feel a surge of annoyance mingled with respect. 'It's a tape recorder.'

'A tape recorder?'

'I record my patient interviews.'

Luke's eyebrows shoot up to his hairline. 'All of them?'

'Yes.' I shrug like it's no big deal. In New York, it's not illegal to record a conversation that you are a part of, even if the other person is not aware of it. 'I don't do anything with the recordings besides remind myself of the last visit if I need to. I use them in place of notes. I don't have an electronic medical record in my home.'

I watch Luke's expression. I brace myself for him to tell me what I'm doing is terribly wrong or threaten to inform my patients about this breach of confidentiality. But when he finally speaks, what he says shocks me. 'You shouldn't use tapes. You should record them digitally.'

'Digitally?'

'Yeah.' He shakes his head. 'I mean, you must have thousands of these tapes. Wouldn't it be better if you saved everything onto your computer?'

'I like tapes.'

'Tapes? Come on. Did I step into a time machine and get magically transported to the eighties?'

The dopey grin on his face makes me smile back. When I first met Luke at the clinic, I found him mildly annoying, even though he was good at what he did. But he's growing on me.

'Tapes are an excellent recording device,' I say. 'And I'd be happy to offer a demonstration.'

'A demonstration?'

'The Dr Adrienne Hale experience.' I wink at him. 'You take a seat on the couch, and I'll show you what I do.'

His smile falters as he glances behind him at my leather sofa. 'On the couch?'

'Yes. It will be fun.'

'*Fun?*'

'Sure. Why not?'

He runs a hand along the arm of the sofa. 'The Dr Adrienne Hale experience, huh?'

'I should tell you, there are many people who pay top dollar for this.'

'Oh, I'll bet.' He looks down at the sofa again. He's reluctant to do this, but he also doesn't want to say no. He just spent his entire evening here. Even though he's a nice guy, he surely has an ulterior motive. 'Fine. Let's do it. Give me the Dr Adrienne Hale experience.'

CHAPTER 24

TRANSCRIPT OF RECORDING

This is my first session with LS, a thirty … ?

LS: 'Thirty-six.'

DH: 'A thirty-six-year-old man who appears normal but is freakishly good with electronics and computers and also apparently carries a hammer around in the back of his trunk. Suspicious'

LS: 'Hey, you should be grateful I had that hammer.'

DH: 'So, Luke, why don't you tell me a little about yourself?'

LS: 'Like what?'

DH: 'Whatever you think is important.'

LS: 'Well. I have a master's in computer science. I've been working in information technology for … well, since I got my master's. I've been helping medical facilities set up their EMR for the last five years.'

DH: 'Do you enjoy the work?'

LS: 'Sure. I mean, it's a job. But it could be worse.'

DH: 'Are you married, Luke?'

LS: 'You know I'm not.'

DH: 'Do I?'

LS: 'Well, I'm not wearing a ring.'

DH: 'Plenty of married men don't wear wedding bands.'

LS: 'Fine. But I'm not married.'

DH: 'Have you ever been married?'

LS: 'Um …'

DH: 'Luke?'

LS: 'Yes. I have.'

DH: 'I see. And how did that end?'

LS: 'She died.'

DH: 'I'm so sorry.'

LS: 'It's … it's fine. It was a long time ago.'

DH: 'Do you want to talk about—'

LS: 'No, I don't want to talk about it. Let's move on, okay?'

DH: 'Fair enough. But I just think—'

LS: 'This was a bad idea. Shut the tape recorder off.'

DH: 'I disagree. We have a lot to explore here.'

LS: 'Really.'

DH: 'Yes. You're a very complex and interesting person, Luke Strauss.'

LS: 'Am I?'

DH: 'Don't laugh. You just gave up your entire evening to do a favour for a woman you hardly even know. And you expected nothing from this woman in return.'

LS: 'I had to do it. She lives in the middle of nowhere. I wouldn't want anything to happen to her.'

DH: 'That's considerate.'

LS: 'I'm a nice guy, I guess. Or a sucker.'

DH: 'You'd only be a sucker if you did it expecting something from her that she didn't intend to deliver.'

LS: 'I don't … I mean, I'm not *expecting* anything. Hoping, I guess.'

DH: 'Hoping for what?'

LS: 'Nothing. Never mind.'

DH: 'No, tell me.'

LS: 'So this woman I helped tonight … you called me complex and interesting, and I don't know if you're right, but this woman, she's all those things. And more. Really smart—like you wouldn't believe. Also, she comes to this low-income clinic on her own free time, and she really cares about the patients there. She acts like it's no big deal, but what she does for them is amazing. They love her.'

DH: 'So you wanted to help her because she helps others?'

LS: 'Yes … I mean, that's part of it, but …'

DH: 'But?'

LS: 'She's interesting and complex and caring and intelligent. But she's also …'

DH: 'What?'

LS: 'She's beautiful.'

DH: 'You think so, do you?'

LS: 'I do. I really do.'

DH: 'I see. So what you're saying is that you have romantic intentions toward this woman?'

LS: 'Uh …'

DH: 'Are you aware that your face is bright red right now?'

LS: 'Ha ha, very amusing. Okay, I … Look, what do you want me to say? Yes. Yes, I like her.'

DH: 'And how does she feel about you?'

LS: 'Until today, I would have said she doesn't like me much. But now I'm not so sure. She's very hard to read.'

DH: 'Is that so?'

LS: 'Yeah. I mean, I've been at her house for two hours, then she gets me on her sofa and does this weird pretend interview, asking me all these questions. And the whole time, I keep thinking, what if I just got up off the sofa and kissed her? How would she react?'

DH: 'Why don't you do it then?'

LS: 'What if she doesn't want me to? What if she slaps me?'

DH: 'I don't think she will'

LS: 'No?'

DH: 'You never know unless you try.'

CHAPTER 25

ADRIENNE

BEFORE

I never expected to end up in bed with Luke Strauss. Dinner? Maybe. A few drinks? Possibly. But not this. It came as a complete surprise.

But not an unpleasant one. Just the opposite. I had thought of myself as the sort of person who could go indefinitely without physical affection, but the second Luke kissed me after I goaded him into it, I realized I was kidding myself. I wanted this. I wanted it so badly that even when he respectfully tried to slow things down, I wouldn't let him.

Whatever you want, Adrienne.

I got exactly what I wanted. A night of passion with a man who surprised me by very much knowing what he was doing. He did a good job installing my security system. He did a better job in the bedroom.

I feel utterly satisfied.

But now it is over. Luke has his arm around my shoulders, and my naked body is pressed against his, and all I can think about is, *How am I going to get him to leave?* It's after midnight—surely he expects to spend the night. I like him, but I don't want him in my bed any more. I don't want him tossing and turning and snoring and trying to cuddle me while I sleep. I need my sleep.

I also sense that it would be tacky to turn to him and say, *Hey, that was fun. How about you run along home now?* I might be stuck with him. The entire night.

'You know what?' Luke murmurs into my hair. 'I'm starving.'

At his words, my stomach growls loud enough for him to hear.

He laughs. 'I guess that means you concur.'

'Do you want to get some food downstairs? We can raid my fridge.'

'Sounds good to me.'

He might not say that when he discovers the meager contents of my refrigerator. But then again, I sense he won't be too bothered. Luke is very agreeable. I haven't decided whether I am fond of that quality about him or not.

Luke climbs out of bed and gathers the clothing that was tossed around the room in a fit of passion. As he's zipping up his pants, he notices that I'm watching him and looks up at me with a grin. For the first time since I saw that video on my phone, I feel a flash of happiness.

That video. EJ. That asshole.

No. Don't think about it. Not now.

Luke throws his partially buttoned shirt over his head but doesn't secure the rest of the buttons. Then he grabs his tie from the floor and lets it hang loose around his neck. I consider getting dressed in my clothes from earlier today like he has, but then I decide to hell with it. I grab my red fleece robe and wrap it around my body.

He smiles in approval. I bought the robe because it's warm, but it has the added bonus of being red. I swear I didn't consider that when I purchased it, but perhaps subconsciously I did.

The contents of the refrigerator are even more abysmal than I feared. I have a loaf of bread, but when Luke picks it up, there's green mold growing at the bottom. There's a bottle of ketchup. There's dry pasta in one of the cupboards but no pasta sauce. Only ketchup.

'I eat out a lot,' I say apologetically. 'I would hope so.'

He opens another cupboard and finds a package of only slightly stale saltines and some peanut butter. It's not exactly the dinner of champions, but it will do. I have a pack of water bottles at the bottom of the fridge, and I retrieve one for myself and hand another to Luke, who is busy making peanut butter and saltine sandwiches.

'Sorry,' I say.

'Don't be sorry.' He pauses to lick peanut butter off the butter knife. 'This was my favourite meal from ages seven through ten.'

I smile to myself, imagining Luke as a freckle-faced second grader. 'I bet you were a cute kid.'

'I was,' he assures me. He slides one of the saltine peanut butter sandwiches over to me. I take a bite—it tastes about as you would think it would. 'I didn't become a handful until I was a teenager.'

I arch an eyebrow. 'You gave your parents a hard time? That's hard to imagine.'

He licks some peanut butter off his upper lip. 'Not exactly. I got into some trouble though. Legal trouble.'

'Legal trouble? Really?'

He hesitates as if considering lying about it even though he just told me it was true. I'm sure Luke Strauss has a tell, but I haven't found it yet. 'Yes.'

'Like what?'

'Hacking.' He winces. 'I thought I was so smart … until I got caught. I got in a shitload of trouble. Luckily, I was a minor and my parents got me a good lawyer. I just did community service, and they made sure it didn't end up on my permanent record.'

'Wow. I'm impressed.'

'Impressed that I was a hacker? Or impressed that I stayed out of jail?'

'Both. But mostly the first.' I crumble a bit of cracker under my fingertips. 'Can you still do it?'

'Do what?'

'Hack into computers.'

He chuckles. 'Maybe, but we are not going to find out. Nobody will ever hire you to do any legit computer work if you get caught doing something like that. I'm old enough to know not to take any stupid chances like that any more.'

I already knew Luke was skilled with computers. But this is an interesting piece of information. I file it away in my brain for later.

'I bet you were perfect when you were a kid,' he comments. 'I bet you were the kind of kid that every adult was in love with. A teacher's pet—am I right?'

'Not exactly.'

His left eyebrow arches up. 'Is that so?'

'A lot of teachers don't like you,' I say, 'when you're smarter than they are.'

Luke stares at me for a second, then he chuckles. 'Yeah, I'll just bet you were.'

I'm pleased that he found my assertion amusing rather than arrogant. It is, after all, simply a fact. Very early on, my intellect exceeded everyone who was tasked to teach me. And a lot of adults indeed resent a child who is smarter than they are.

A lot of parents do as well.

I brace myself for more questions about my childhood and family, but they never come. Instead, we sit quietly in my kitchen, chewing our saltine peanut butter sandwiches. Even if I wanted to make conversation, it would be hard with all the peanut butter stuck to the roof of my mouth. Perhaps that is why Luke stopped asking questions and not out of respect for my privacy. He looks around the house as we eat, a slightly amazed look on his face.

'Big place you got here,' he finally says. 'Yes, it's just me.'

He runs his tongue over his teeth. 'I didn't ask.'

'You didn't have to.' I drum my fingers against the kitchen table. 'People look at this house and assume I must live here with a husband and children. And when I defy that expectation, it upsets them. People dislike when things don't meet their expectations.'

'Well,' he says, 'I want you to know that you *exceed* my expectations.'

I allow myself a smile. 'Do I?'

'You do. And also, I'm pretty glad you don't have a husband. Obviously.'

I shift my weight in the wooden kitchen chair. 'How about you? You told me you used to be married.'

It's amazing the way Luke completely shuts down when I bring up his previous marriage. That's exactly what happened when I was trying to interview him earlier. His eyes wall off and his lips set into a straight line. 'I don't want to talk about it.'

'I see.'

He's not being fair. He's thirty-six years old and a widower. He must realize that such a revelation is enough to make people wonder. How do you lose your wife at such a young age?

He sees my expression and lets out a sigh. 'She was in an accident. It was … awful. And I hope this doesn't sound cold, but it's honestly the last thing I want to think about when I'm here with you.'

'I understand.' And I do. It's not like it would be better if Luke was going on and on about his dead wife. He claims he's over it, and I believe that. But I still can't help but wonder. What sort of accident was it? Was he involved?

In any case, I'm not going to find out the answers to my questions tonight.

Between me and Luke, we polish off the rest of the saltines and peanut butter. I glance at the clock on the microwave—it's nearly one in the morning. Even though he put his clothes back on, his shirt is still mostly unbuttoned. He lives all the way in the Bronx, and he's never going to want to make the hike back to his apartment this late. He's going to want to stay the night.

He'll probably want to cuddle all night. A cold sweat breaks out on the back of my neck.

'So.' I clear my throat. 'This was nice.'

'Yeah.' A smile plays on his lips. 'It really was.'

'I wouldn't mind doing it again sometime,' I say. That part is true. But next time at his place so I could leave when it's over.

'I'm on board.'

'Any other time. Just ... you know, text me.'

'I will.'

'Yes. So.'

A long silence hangs between us. Finally, Luke breaks the silence. By bursting out laughing.

I stare at him, affronted. 'What's so funny?'

He wipes his eyes. He's laughing so hard there are tears. 'You want me to leave so badly, but you're too nice to say it.'

'Well ...' I fold my arms across my bare chest. 'I'm just used to sleeping alone. And don't you prefer your own bed too?'

'I absolutely do.' He leans forward to brush his lips against mine. 'Honestly, I've got to be at another hospital in the city tomorrow morning, and I wasn't looking forward to running home at the crack of dawn to shower and get fresh clothes. I would've stayed if you wanted me to, but I'm good with going home.'

My entire body sags with relief. 'Thank you.'

'But'—he holds up a finger—'you have to let me take you out to dinner.'

'I'm the one who owes *you* dinner, remember?'

'Except no way. I want to take *you* out to dinner.'

From an evolutionary perspective, females are more reproductively valuable than males. After all, we can only carry one pregnancy at a time while men can spread their seed more freely. As a result, male mammals must 'earn' female reproductive access by offering gifts. It's certainly not unique to humans, although I would say sheep or cows rarely find themselves in this particular conundrum.

From a social psychological standpoint, traditional gender roles are often internalized for men. They feel obligated to make decisions and take control while women follow. By setting a precedent such as paying for a meal on a first date, the man is establishing himself as the dominant leader in the relationship and relegates the woman to the passive role.

I consider explaining all this to Luke, but then he leans back in the kitchen chair, which groans under his weight. 'I'll stay here *all night* if I have to, Adrienne.'

Fine. If he wants it that badly, I will not argue. Despite my distaste at the prospect of falling into traditional gender roles, I'm a little flattered. 'All right then. You may take me out to dinner.'

I walk Luke to the front door. Just before he leaves, he grabs me one last time and kisses me. It's a lovely kiss that makes me tingle down to my toes. I can't wait to see him again.

And as he heads out the door, the thought flits through my head that maybe Luke could help me out with the EJ problem.

CHAPTER 26

TRICIA

PRESENT DAY

He liked her. He really liked her.

I can hear it in his voice. This was obviously recorded before they were dating, and he just had a crush on her. It's so sweet you could almost throw up. It sounds like she let him kiss her. And then some.

Luke doesn't sound like a killer. He sounds like a decent guy, if a bit nerdy. His voice isn't dripping with evil like EJ's. But of course, this was at the beginning of their relationship. A lot can change. Did she do something to him that made him hate her? She must have.

I shiver in Dr Hale's leather chair. The blouse I'm wearing is paper thin and not nearly warm enough, even with the heat on. Maybe I can get Ethan to turn the heat up a bit. He never showed me exactly how he figured out how to turn it on in the first place. I don't even know where the heating system is. It could be practically anywhere in this giant house. I'm impressed he figured it out, having never been here before.

I eject the LUKE tape from the tape recorder and stuff it back in the bottom drawer. Then I leave the office and head upstairs to find Ethan.

It's amazing how different it looks in the hallway of the second floor when the sun is up. It was nothing short of terrifying last night, but now it doesn't seem so bad. I'm still reluctant to live here, but it wouldn't be the worst thing in the world. The windows make it bright and cheery, although they illuminate every crack and imperfection in the wall.

And they illuminate one other thing: A pull cord hanging from the ceiling.

I don't know how I missed it last night. I guess it makes sense since the hallway was so dark and the cord isn't exactly easy to see. I can now see that the cord attaches to a rectangle on the ceiling.

It's a passage to the attic.

Of course! I remember now in Judy's description of the house on the website she mentioned 'an attic perfect for storage.' But somehow it didn't even occur to me last night. When we checked all the rooms on the second floor, I assumed that we had covered all our bases in terms of where somebody could go.

But there was another option. The attic.

I reach up and tug on the cord. Nothing happens. I tug harder, and this time I hear a click, and the rectangle swings open. There is a ladder folded up inside, and when I pull on it, it comes down, ending at my feet.

I glance at the room next to me—the door is shut tight. That must be where Ethan is working. I'd like to ask him to check the attic, but I have a feeling he won't be too excited about that. He already seemed exasperated with me after I made him check every room on the floor. And I only made things worse when I started freaking out in the middle of the night. He's already calling me 'nutty' and blaming pregnancy hormones.

I squint up into the opening of the attic. It doesn't look too dark up there. There are so many windows, there's no way somebody could hide up there and jump out at me. I could check it out myself. And if I spot anything upsetting, I'll yell for Ethan. He'll hear me easily—the walls are thin in this house.

I grab one of the rungs of the ladder, putting my weight on it to test its stability. It seems stable—and it's not like I weigh a ton. I place one of my feet on the bottom rung, then the other foot. Before I can talk myself out of it, I start climbing the ladder carefully. I've got to see what's in this attic.

A few seconds later, I reach the top of the ladder. I hesitate for a split second, then I stick my head through the opening. And I look around. It looks like …

An attic.

A completely normal, unremarkable attic. In one corner, there's a bunch of dusty cardboard boxes, and in the next corner, there's a plastic Christmas tree that looks like it's seen better days. I imagine the woman with the intense green eyes struggling to get that bulky Christmas tree out of the attic and into her living room, and I almost laugh. It makes the painting a little less scary.

I climb the rest of the way into the attic, satisfied that there isn't anyone waiting to pounce on me in here. The ceiling is much lower here—a stark contrast to the high ceilings on the first floor. If I stretch, I could probably touch it.

Most of the attic is filled with boxes. Dusty boxes. I'm surprised nobody cleared it out at some point. I wonder if the police went through the boxes in their search to find her. Unlike the hidden room of tapes, this stuff is all in plain sight.

I pace around the small space, wondering if there's some hidden chamber up here as well. There aren't any bookcases anyway. I walk over to a stack of boxes and blow some dust off the top box. It's labelled in permanent black marker in Adrienne Hale's now familiar handwriting: ornaments.

I lift the box and shake it. Sure enough, ornaments rattle inside the box.

I wonder what will become of all the stuff in the attic if we were to buy the house. Not that I'm seriously considering such a thing, but would all this stuff get left behind? Would they expect us to sort through Dr Hale's belongings? Doesn't she have family who could do that?

Maybe she doesn't though. It didn't seem like anyone was in any hurry to claim any of her furniture. The seller of the house is listed as a bank—I am assuming they fore closed on the property after she disappeared.

As I'm dropping the box of ornaments back in the pile, I notice something stuck behind the boxes. Something made of fabric. I pull it out and suck in a breath when I realize what I've found.

It's a sleeping bag.

There's nothing that disturbing about finding a sleeping bag in somebody's attic. On the contrary, it's what you might expect to find. But the disturbing part is that everything in this attic is covered in a layer of dust. But the sleeping bag isn't. The sleeping bag is clean. Recently laundered.

There's also a pillow stuck back there, which seems to be in the same condition. There's a pillowcase on it, and it's all clean. It's not covered in dirt and dust like everything else in the attic. There's only one conclusion I can draw.

Somebody was using the sleeping bag very recently.

CHAPTER 27

I drop the sleeping bag and pillow where I found them, my heart pounding. I've got to get out of this attic. Because I'm not sure I'm alone in here any more.

I take brisk steps to the trapdoor. My hands are trembling so hard, I'm afraid I'm going to slip and fall through the door. I have to take a few deep breaths to calm myself down. Nobody is going to attack me in this attic. Not when Ethan is within earshot.

By some miracle, I make it down the stairs to the second level without falling. As soon as my feet touch the floor, I turn to the bedroom door that's closed and start pounding on it. After a second, I realize it probably isn't locked, so I try the doorknob, and it twists under my hand.

'Tricia?'

Ethan is sitting at the desk in the room, his hands positioned over the keyboard of his laptop. He looks shocked to see me standing there.

'There's someone in the attic!' I gasp.

Ethan leaps to his feet. '*What?*'

'I ...' I'm starting to hyperventilate. My breaths are coming too quickly. Ethan rounds the desk and puts his arm around me. 'There's a ...'

He squeezes my body close to his—protectively. 'A man?'

I shake my head. 'A sleeping bag.'

'A ...' His protective grip on my shoulders loosens slightly. 'A sleeping bag?'

'Yes! And it's clean!'

'I ... I don't get it, Tricia.'

I shrug off his embrace, upset that he doesn't seem concerned any more. 'Somebody is sleeping in the attic!' He rubs the growing stubble on his chin. At home, he usually shaves every morning. 'Just because there's a sleeping bag up there, it doesn't mean somebody is sleeping in the attic. People keep sleeping bags in the attic.'

'But it's clean!' I'm desperate to make him understand. 'Everything in this house is so dusty, but the sleeping bag has been recently used. It's not dusty.'

'Maybe it was under something that was keeping it from getting dusty?'

I glare at him.

'I'm sorry, Tricia,' he sighs. 'I just don't think a sleeping bag in the attic is evidence that there's some stranger in the house. We haven't seen anyone here. I haven't seen any signs that there's another person here.'

'Are you kidding me? There have been a zillion signs that there's somebody here! There was a light on upstairs that mysteriously turned off. All that food in the fridge.

The footprints on the floor. I heard a crash when I was downstairs. And the painting that moved …'

I stop talking because it's obvious from the look on Ethan's face that nothing I'm saying is convincing him even a little bit.

'Fine,' I grunt. 'Don't believe me.'

'It's not that I don't believe you …'

'Hmm. Isn't that exactly what this is?'

'I just think …' He reaches for me again, and I reluctantly allow him to put his arm around my shoulders. 'You're under a lot of stress right now. I mean, we're stranded here without phone service. And your body is in the middle of making an entire other person. I don't blame you for feeling tense. Also …' He rubs his hand up and down my arm, which I now realize is covered in goose bumps. 'You're freezing.'

With the excitement of finding that sleeping bag in the attic, I forgot all about the reason I came up here. 'It's really cold in this house.'

He nods. 'I know. Unfortunately, I don't know how much warmer it's going to get. The insulation is terrible. We're going to have to put in some major funds to get it fixed.'

Great. My teeth are on the verge of chattering. 'So what are we supposed to do? Wear our coats?'

'Well …' He glances down the hallway. 'The master bedroom has an entire walk-in closet filled with clothing. There's got to be some warm stuff in there that's more comfortable than wearing your coat around the house.'

I grit my chattering teeth. 'I am *not* wearing a dead woman's clothing.'

'All right, but you have two choices. Either wear her clothing, or wear your coat. Or be cold, I guess.'

I hate the idea of going through Adrienne Hale's closet and scavenging for clothing. But it's not comfortable to sit around indoors in my coat. Maybe I am being silly. I could grab something from the back of the closet. Something she rarely wore. Hell, I'm willing to bet a woman like that probably has a few outfits still with price tags on them.

'Fine,' I grumble. 'I'll check the closet.'

Ethan kisses me on the top of my head. 'Good. And after you find something warm to wear, we can go downstairs and have lunch.'

'Not bologna again. Please.'

He flashes a crooked smile. 'I saw turkey too.'

I am going to be so sick of cold cuts by the time we get out of here.

Ethan returns to his laptop while I walk down the hall to the master bedroom. I will take *one sweater* from her closet and that's it. And I'm just borrowing it. I'm going to put it back before we leave here. In the exact condition I found it.

When I return to Dr Hale's walk-in closet, it's even more stuffed with clothing than I remember. I have a lot of clothes—I'm not going to lie—but her clothes are *classy*. Everything she wears is at the height of fashion. And not just that—she doesn't own anything casual. I looked through some of her drawers last night, and it seemed like the lady didn't even own a pair of blue jeans.

I would wager that there isn't one piece of clothing in this closet that cost less than two hundred dollars.

I had intended to find something in the back of her closet that she rarely wore, but my attention goes back to that white cashmere sweater I had been slobbering over last night. I love cashmere. I mean, everyone does. What sort of freak doesn't like cashmere?

And the sweater is so white. Like unblemished snow. I grab the sweater and pull it off the hanger. I throw it over my head, almost groaning in ecstasy at how nice the fabric feels against my skin. I love cashmere.

Okay, I didn't do exactly what I said I was going to do. But it's almost a crime for a sweater like this to be sitting in a closet, never worn. It's *begging* to be worn. *Crying* to be worn.

And it's not like Adrienne Hale is going to come back here and want to wear the sweater, for God's sake.

CHAPTER 28

ADRIENNE

BEFORE

I watch Luke expertly chopping vegetables on my kitchen counter. I might be hopeless in the kitchen, but he's an excellent cook. We still get takeout plenty, but he likes to cook for me on the nights he's here. Which are becoming more and more frequent.

Luke and I have been dating for four months. It's a record for me. After a month of dating, my anxiety abated to the point where I finally consented to let him spend the night. And now he's here three or four nights a week. There are ground rules of course. He has to stay on his side of the bed—no cuddling in the middle of the night. And if I'm not feeling in the mood to have company, he has to leave without argument. The first month, that happened as often as not. But I haven't asked him to leave in weeks. The truth is, I'm growing to enjoy sharing a bed with him. On the nights he's at his own apartment, I look at the empty spot on what has now become his side of the bed (the left), and I feel an ache in my chest.

'It smells delicious,' I comment.

Luke picks up a long-handled spoon and stirs the sauce that has been simmering on the stove for the last twenty minutes. He's sexy when he's cooking, maybe because he's so skilled at it. 'It's a new recipe. You're going to love it.'

'I'm sure I will. I love everything you make.' And I love *you*.

The thought pops into my head against my will.

Those three words keep cropping up and taunting me. I can't say that to him. First of all, he hasn't said it to me. And even if he did, I still don't think I could say it. I'm not even sure it's true.

I've never told a man that I love him before. It seems odd, I'm sure, given my age. Men have told me they love me before, and I have not said it back. Men, compared with women, are statistically much faster to express sentiments of love, despite stereotypes to the contrary. I have counselled patients on this before, and I always advise them you should never say 'I love you' to another person unless that is what you're feeling.

I have never told a man that I love him because I have never felt that I loved any of my prior significant others.

If I spoke to a therapist about it, I'm sure they would have a lot to say about the lack of intimacy in my life. I was never close with my parents. My father was a mail carrier, and my mother worked as a receptionist. Neither of them attended college, much less obtained multiple advanced degrees. They never quite knew what to make of me.

When I was younger, I was convinced I had been switched with another child at birth. Or perhaps adopted, based on the fact that my mother was told in her twenties that she would never bear children, and I was conceived as a miracle baby. I dreamed about someday being reunited with my biological parents, who would finally understand me. But of course, this was all a childish fantasy. Instead, my mother developed ovarian cancer when I was in college. My father, who never understood the purpose of college to begin with, pressured me to drop out to help him care for her during a brutal course of chemotherapy. I refused, and she died almost exactly one year after her diagnosis. Six months after losing the love of his life, my father died of a heart attack.

Luke has also experienced loss. Even though he doesn't like to talk about it, I have weaseled some details out of him about his late wife. They were college sweet-hearts. There was a car accident. She died instantly.

When he told me the story about the car accident, he spoke in a monotone, as if blocking off his emotions. I asked him if he ever saw a therapist after the accident, and he told me yes, but then he wouldn't talk about it any more.

In some ways though, it's a relief he won't talk about his former marriage. Because if he were to open up about it to me, he might expect me to do the same about the loss of my parents. And I do not have any desire to do so. I'd rather not admit to him that my parents never cared for me and that the feeling was mutual.

'Can you babysit the stove for a few minutes?' Luke asks me.

I bristle. In a few minutes, I could easily destroy this meal. 'Why?'

'I want to grab a change of clothes from my car. I'm not going to want to run out there later.'

'Oh.'

'You know …' He gives me a pointed look. 'I don't *have* to live like a nomad all the time.'

I take a step back, my heart pounding. Does he want to move in with me? He's been here so frequently lately, but I can't contemplate such a thing. Even though I haven't asked him to leave in a long time, the option is there. We have our own space. If he moved in, he would be here all the time. Yes, it's a big house, but it suddenly feels very small.

'Relax, Adrienne,' he says quickly. 'I don't want to move in. I'm just saying, maybe you could clear out a drawer for me or something. You know?'

'Oh.' My breathing slows. 'Yes. I could do that.

I … I'm sorry. I didn't mean to …'

'It's okay.' He puts down the spoon in his hand and pulls me closer to him so he can kiss me. One of those lingering kisses that makes my whole body tingle. He still gets to me, even after four months. 'I know you're nuts It's one of the things I love about you.'

He's doing it too. Flirting with the word 'love.' *I love your sauce. I love that you're nuts.* He's going to say it to me—I can see it all over his face. It's just a matter of time.

While he's kissing me, a chime comes from the front door. The doorbell. At eight thirty in the evening.

'Who the hell is that?' Luke asks.

I grab my phone from where I left it on the kitchen counter. I bring up the camera app to see who's at the front door. My stomach sinks. It's EJ.

The doorbell rings again.

Luke turns to answer the door, but I grab his arm. 'Don't answer it.'

He frowns. 'Who is it?'

'A patient. Just ignore it. He'll go away.'

Luke's forehead creases. 'Why is one of your patients ringing the doorbell at eight o'clock in the evening?'

'It's fine.' I swallow. 'He has some boundary issues. It's better to ignore him.'

The doorbell rings again, and Luke's face darkens. 'It's not fine. I'll go tell him that this is not appropriate and he should leave you alone.'

'No. *No.*' Before Luke can leave the kitchen, I grab his arm, my phone still gripped in my other hand. My fingernails dig into his skin. 'Trust me on this. Just ignore him, and he'll go away. I promise.'

I don't let go of his arm until he relaxes. He lets out a sigh. 'Fine. You're the shrink. You know what's best.'

The doorbell doesn't ring again, but I'm not kidding myself that EJ has gone away. I look down at the screen of my phone while Luke tends to our dinner. After a few seconds, the message appears on the screen:

I know you're home.

I glance up at Luke, then type my response: *I'm busy.*

Busy with your boyfriend?

Of course EJ would know about Luke. I could never keep any relationship of mine a secret from him. Usually though, when he shows up late at night, he picks nights when Luke isn't here. He's becoming bolder.

I need an appointment with you, Dr Hale.

I'm busy now. I can see you tomorrow afternoon.

No. Tomorrow morning.

I bite down on my lower lip. He always does this. He pushes the boundaries to see what he can make me do. Will he go public with that video just because I refuse to see him in the morning instead of the afternoon? I assume not. But I don't know for sure. And he's so impulsive, he might do it in a moment of rage. So I must play the game. I am at his whim. I promised him weekly appointments, but it's become two or three times a week. They are not productive appointments. Often, he makes me listen to him describe his sexual exploits in disgusting detail. Worst of all, there's always the suggestion that I might want to join in. But he hasn't forced the issue.

Yet.

Fine, I type. *Tomorrow morning at 10. Please be prompt.*

I always am.

CHAPTER 29

TRANSCRIPT OF RECORDING

This is session #179 with EJ, a twenty-nine-year-old man with narcissistic personality disorder.

EJ: 'Thanks for seeing me on such short notice, Doc.'
DH: 'I didn't have much of a choice, did I?'
EJ: 'Don't say it like that. You like our appointments as much as I do.'
DH: 'What can I help you with today?'
EJ: 'Here's the thing. Yesterday I went for a run. That was your advice, that I should be more active. So I was trying to do what you suggested.'
DH: 'That's great.'
EJ: 'Yeah, except when I was running, I twisted my knee.'
DH: 'That's unfortunate.'
EJ: 'It hurts a lot. On a scale of one to ten, the pain is like a twelve.'
DH: 'You didn't seem to be limping.'

EJ: 'It's not that kind of pain. Trust me, it hurts a lot. Deep inside.'
DH: 'I'm sorry to hear that.'
EJ: 'So maybe you can help me out. Especially since it's your fault. I mean, you're the one who told me to go running.'
DH: 'I'm afraid I don't know much about knee pain. Perhaps you should make an appointment with your primary care doctor?'
EJ: 'I don't have a primary care doctor.'
DH: 'Urgent care then.'
EJ: 'Well, I don't think it's anything serious. I just need something for the pain. I was hoping you could prescribe me some oxycodone.'
DH: 'Oxy …'
EJ: 'Like thirty tablets should do it. I was thinking ten milligram tabs.'
DH: 'If you have a knee injury, you should see a specialist who treats that. I'm a psychiatrist. I am not trained to manage knee pain.'
EJ: 'Well, you went to medical school, didn't you?'
DH: 'Yes, but that was a long time ago.'
EJ: 'It doesn't matter. My knee is fine. I just need some oxycodone to get through it. Like I said, thirty tablets should be perfect.'
DH: 'I can't just give you a prescription for a narcotic. These medications are controlled.'
EJ: 'Don't give me that bullshit. You prescribe stuff way stronger than oxycodone.'
DH: 'Psychiatric medications. Not narcotics. I can't give you thirty tablets of oxycodone. I could get in trouble.'

EJ: 'More or less trouble than if a video came out of you slashing someone's tires?'

DH: 'I ...'

EJ: 'Like I said, thirty tablets should be fine. I won't sell them or anything. I just want to get through this knee pain. Have pity on me, Doc.'

DH: 'I'll give you twenty tablets. Five milligrams each.'

EJ: 'I didn't realize this was a negotiation.'

DH: 'I could lose my license.'

EJ: 'Thirty tablets. You could do the five-milligram ones if that makes you feel better.'

DH: 'Fine. But this is the only time.'

EJ: 'Right. Of course, Doc. I'm not going to ask you for oxycodone again. I mean, unless I hurt my knee again.'

CHAPTER 30

TRICIA

PRESENT DAY

Ethan is making us lunch. I said I would do it, because he has made the last two meals, but he's so insistent.

'You're pregnant. I have to take care of you.'

He's making me feel silly for having waited so long to tell him about the baby.

He gets the packet of turkey out of the refrigerator. But instead of putting it on the bread, he places the pieces on a plate and sticks them in the microwave. Then he heats it up for thirty seconds.

'What are you doing?' I ask, baffled.

'Pregnant women aren't supposed to eat cold cuts,' he explains. 'They have to be heated. To kill the bacteria.'

'Really?'

He nods solemnly. 'I read it's very serious. You could get really sick.'

'Oh ...' I think back to the bologna sandwich I ate earlier. And I might have eaten a roast beef sandwich earlier in the week. God, I need to be more careful. This pregnancy thing is so tricky. 'I'm glad you checked. But how did you know that? We don't have any internet.'

He hesitates for a beat. 'I didn't read it today, obviously. I read it before. Like a long time ago. I just remembered it.'

'Oh.'

I don't know why my husband would have been reading about things pregnant women should and shouldn't do years ago. But I'm not going to question him. Maybe he read it in an article and it stuck in his mind. That happens to me sometimes. That's how I learned that there are earthquakes on the moon. And they're called moonquakes. 'I wonder if you're having a girl or a boy,' he muses as he pulls the heated turkey out of the microwave. 'I have a feeling it's a girl.'

'Based on what?'

I lift my shoulders. 'I don't know. It's just this feeling I have.'

He smiles indulgently. Ethan might be a nice guy, but he is not spiritual. He believes in science and facts and is the kind of person who would roll his eyes over me telling him I have a *feeling* about the gender of our child.

'If it's a girl,' I say, 'we could name her after your mother. And if it's a boy, we could name him after your dad.' It's like a curtain has dropped over Ethan's face. He plops a lump of mayonnaise on one of the sandwiches without even bothering to spread it out. 'My parents and I weren't close.'

I frown at the edge that has crept into his voice. 'Why not?'

'We just weren't.' 'Did you fight?'

He picks up a knife from the block and starts slicing the sandwiches. 'Sometimes. I don't know.'

'What did you fight about?'

'I don't remember.'

'You must remember *something* about it ...'

Ethan slams the knife down on the counter loud enough that I jump. 'I *said* I don't remember, Tricia.'

I back away from the counter. 'I'm sorry. I didn't mean to upset you.'

He looks up at me, his crystal-blue eyes flashing. 'Why do you always have to be so damn *curious* about everything? Why do you have to know everything about everyone?'

'I just ...' I wring my hands together. 'I don't have to know everything about everyone. I just want to know about *you*. Because you're my husband, and I love you.'

I don't know why it's so hard for him to wrap his head around this. I mean, Ethan has met every member of my family—even my great-aunt Bertha, who is ninety-nine years old, was at our wedding. And I have met *nobody* from his family. Not even one person.

Is it so wrong to be curious where he came from?

After all, he's going to be the father of my child.

'I don't want to talk about my parents.' His voice is quiet now but firm. 'It ... it brings back bad memories, okay? I want to move forward ... with you. I don't want to look backward.'

'Okay,' I say. 'I understand.'

Ethan carries the plates containing our turkey sandwiches to the kitchen table. I join him, but I'm still feeling wary after that outburst. The two of us eat our sandwiches, but we're quieter than we usually are during meals. Obviously, there are some topics that Ethan feels he can't talk about with me. But he's wrong. I need him to see that he can tell me anything. *Anything*.

Although perhaps not at this very moment, when we're trapped in an isolated house with no way out in the foreseeable future.

'How are we going to get out of here?' I blurt out. 'Good question.' Ethan glances out one of the picture windows. The blanket of white is still unblemished. 'I would have thought Judy would try to send somebody for us by now.'

'What if she doesn't realize we're here?' I chew on a lump of the turkey sandwich. The microwave dried it out, and the mayonnaise doesn't help that much. 'Maybe she texted to tell us she wasn't coming and she just assumes we didn't show either?'

He rakes a hand through his golden hair. 'Yeah, that's a possibility. But by Monday, people will start missing us. Your family, my coworkers ... They're going to figure out we're gone.'

'Monday!' I burst out. 'You mean we have to stay here another night?'

'Is it that big a deal?'

Last night, I got one of the least restful nights of sleep I've had in a long time. So no, I'm not excited to spend another night here.

And then Ethan makes it way worse when he adds, 'After all, we're going to be living here soon.'

I cough into my free hand. 'Um, about that ...' His eyebrows fly up. 'What?'

How can I tell him? How can I shoot down his dream house? But I can't *live* here, can I? I'd have nightmares every night until I'd eventually be murdered in my sleep— strangled to death by a white cashmere sweater.

'There are so many other houses out there,' I say. 'I just don't want to jump at this one and miss out on something better.'

'Better? Tricia, we've been looking at houses for months. There's *nothing* better. Everything out there is crap.'

He isn't completely wrong. This is the nicest house we've seen so far, and the price is so reasonable. But I can't live here. I just *can't*.

'I'll think about it,' I mumble.

'I just think it's so perfect.' He shows off a row of his perfect, white teeth. Years of braces, I'm sure. But I can't ask him, because that would be asking about his past, and apparently, I'm not allowed to do that. 'I can just picture us growing old and raising our children here. Can't you?'

'Yes,' I lie. 'I can.'

CHAPTER 31

TRANSCRIPT OF RECORDING

This is session #183 with PL, a twenty-seven-year-old female experiencing PTSD after surviving an extremely traumatic incident but who has largely recovered.

PL: 'Dr Hale, I hope this isn't inappropriate, but I brought you a little present. Well, actually, a big present.'

DH: 'Oh. Oh my.'

PL: 'It was my mother's idea. She always says happiness doesn't result from what we get but from what we give.'

DH: 'Oh. Yes.'

PL: 'So she commissioned this artist, and we used the photograph on the back of your book. I hope it's not too big! She thought it would look great over your mantel.'

DH: 'Um. No, it's … very nice.'

PL: 'Are you sure you like it? You don't have to hang it up. You could just stash it in your basement or something.'

DH: 'No, I like it. I'll hang it up.'

PL: 'We just wanted to do something for you. I was such a mess when I started seeing you. I couldn't sleep. I couldn't think straight. You helped me so much.'

DH: 'What you went through was traumatic. You watched three of the people closest to you murdered right in front of you. It just proves how strong you are.'

PL: 'I feel strong now. I didn't always. Thank you for that.'

DH: 'Yes. You're welcome.'

PL: 'And I'm glad you could include it in your new book. I'm honoured. I hope my story inspires other people.'

DH: 'Yes …'

PL: 'After all this time, I'm finally able to move on. I'm dating again. I'm sleeping well. I do still feel a touch of guilt that I get to continue living my life while the others can't. Is that normal? Will it ever go away?'

DH: 'Mmm.'

PL: 'Dr Hale?'

DH: 'Oh. Um, yes, I think … Yes, it's a good idea. Uhhuh. So … you're sleeping okay then?'

PL: 'Dr Hale?'

DH: 'Yes?'

PL: 'I know it sounds weird me asking this, but are you okay?'

DH: 'Me? Yes, I'm fine.'

PL: 'You look … I'm sorry, but you just look a little pale. And you zoned out there for a minute. Usually you're not like that. You always listen to everything I say.'

DH: 'I'm fine. Really. Just a little … I'm fine. I promise. And I love the painting. In fact, I'm going to hang it up on my mantel right after you leave.'

CHAPTER 32

ADRIENNE

BEFORE

As I lie in Luke's arms, I can't stop thinking about the prescription I wrote for EJ.

I thought spending the evening with Luke would take my mind off of it. And it did for a little while. Luke is good at getting me to laugh, even when I'm in a terrible mood. But tonight is a lost cause. EJ claimed it would be the only prescription he would ask of me, but he was lying. I knew it without even seeing the twitching under his right eye.

He will keep asking for more and more. Pushing me harder and harder.

I have to stop him.

Luke squeezes my shoulders, pulling me closer to his warm body. I try to banish thoughts of EJ from my head and enjoy lying next to Luke. I cleared out a drawer for him a few days ago, and as he filled it with his clothing, the thought occurred to me that it might not be so bad if he were living with me. It would be nice to have him around all the time.

Not now. But maybe someday.

'That portrait of you is so great,' he comments. 'It looks just like you.'

It was funny the way Luke's mouth dropped open when he saw the almost comically large portrait of me that I hung over the mantel. I hung it there partially to make him laugh. But I also did it for my patient. Her traumatic experience formed the crux of my newest book. She's made a lot of progress with me, and I suspect we will conclude our sessions soon.

'You don't think it's too gigantic?' I ask.

'No way!' He squeezes me again. 'It's larger than life. Like you.'

'I'm glad you like it.'

'I love it.' His lips press against my forehead as he holds me close to his body. 'And also, I love … you.'

There it is. The three words we've both been skirting around for the last several weeks. He finally cracked and said it like I knew he would. I've heard those words said to me several times before, but this time, I do something completely unexpected and inappropriate and unlike me.

I burst into tears.

Luke is shaken by my reaction. He pulls away from me, struggling to sit up in my king-size bed. 'Hey,' he says. 'Hey. Don't cry.'

'I'm not crying,' I say pointlessly as I swipe a hand over my leaky eyes. 'I'm fine.'

'I didn't say it because …' He grabs my hand. 'Look, Adrienne, I didn't say it to upset you. You don't have to say it back. I was just feeling it right then, so I said it. And I'm not sorry I did, but it doesn't change anything. I just … I wanted you to know. But I'm not hurt if you don't say it back. I promise.'

He's so good. He's so sweet. I wish I could be happy with him. I wish my life weren't so complicated.

'I'm not crying because of … of that.' I wipe my nose with the back of my hand, wishing I had a tissue. And then, magically, Luke produces a tissue for me, which I accept gratefully. 'It's something else. I have a problem. It has nothing to do with you.'

'The intimacy issue?'

I look up sharply. '*No*. Not that kind of problem.'

He rubs his jaw. He shaves every morning now because he knows I like him better that way, but it's almost bedtime, and he has a rough stubble on his chin. 'Okay, I'm sorry. I just … What kind of problem?'

'I … I'm being blackmailed. By a patient.'

Luke's jaw goes slack. He looks even more stunned than he was by the giant portrait over the mantel. '*Blackmailed*?'

I nod.

'Jesus Christ.' He shakes his head. 'Is this that guy who has been showing up in the middle of the night and texting you all the time?'

I nod again.

He rakes a shaky hand through his short hair. 'Jesus,' he says again. 'I can't believe that … What is he blackmailing you over?'

'He has a video of me. It could wreck my career.' His eyes widen. 'A video?'

'It's not sexual,' I say before he can let his imagination run wild. 'But it's something I'm not proud of.'

'It's really that bad?'

I swallow. 'Yes. It is. And he's holding it over me.

There's nothing I can do about it. Unless ...'

'Unless what?'

'Well ...' My palms feel sweaty. I wipe them on the blanket next to me. 'You said when you were in high school, you used to be pretty good at hacking into computers, right?'

Luke is silent for a moment as he narrows his eyes at me. 'Yes ...'

'Maybe you could find the video for me and ... delete it.'

He pulls away from me, his eyes still wary. 'I can't do that.'

'Why not? You said you know how.'

'It's not that simple. I can't just hack into some random guy's home computer and delete a video. Maybe if I were in his house ...'

'And what if I could get you into his house?'

He inhales sharply. 'Adrienne, what's on that video?'

'Something bad, okay?' A fresh wave of tears rises to the surface. 'Can't you just trust me and help me? I *need* you, Luke. You're the only one who can help me with this.'

He leans forward in the bed and rubs his temples with his fingertips. He doesn't like what I'm asking him, but I already know he's going to say yes. He has never said no to anything I have asked of him. I might be falling for him, but he has fallen far harder for me.

'So what do you want me to do exactly?' he finally asks.

I sit up straighter in bed. 'I'll get you his apartment keys. You go to his house, get into his computer, and delete any traces of the video.'

'And how are you going to get his keys?'

'Let me worry about that.'

'You know ...' He lifts his eyes. 'Even if we delete it from his phone and I somehow get into his computer and find the video there and delete any traces of it, he may still have another copy somewhere else.'

'I don't think he does.' I know EJ, and he's not organized enough to do something like that.

He drops his head back against the pillow. 'I don't know about this, Adrienne. We could get in a lot of trouble.'

'Please help me, Luke.' I reach for his hand, lacing my fingers into his palm. His hand is so much larger and warmer than mine. 'You're the only one who can help me. I need you. I...I love you.'

It's a cheap trick. He told me he loved me, and I'm only saying it back now that I need something from him. I do love him, I really do, but the timing of my declaration is more than suspicious.

But amazingly, my shameless tactic works. His face softens, and that guarded expression fades away. He squeezes my hand in his.

'Okay,' he says. 'I'll do it.'

CHAPTER 33

TRANSCRIPT OF RECORDING

This is session #181 with EJ, a twenty-nine-year-old man with narcissistic personality disorder.

DH: 'I'm so sorry I had to keep you waiting today.' **EJ:** 'That's okay, Doc. I appreciate you leaving the bottle of Cheval Blanc on the coffee table. You know that's my favourite, right? Best doctor's waiting room in the whole damn town.'

DH: 'I knew you'd appreciate it.'

EJ: 'What can I say? I appreciate a good bottle of wine. What year was it?'

DH: 'It's 1948.'

EJ: 'Wow. You spare no expense.'

DH: 'You're paying enough to be here. Well, not *you* Any more. But other people do.'

EJ: 'Yeah. Too bad ...'

DH: 'Excuse me?'

EJ: 'Sorry, I ... I just got this weird light-headed feeling. Like the whole room was spinning or something.'

DH: 'How many glasses of wine did you have?'
EJ: 'Dunno. I just drank it out of the bottle.'
DH: 'All of it?'
EJ: 'Yeah.'
DH: 'Good.'
EJ: 'What?'
DH: 'Nothing. Never mind. Are you okay?'
EJ: 'I, uh … Doc, I feel …'
DH: 'Are you okay?'

CHAPTER 34

ADRIENNE

BEFORE

EJ is unconscious.

It happened quickly. So quickly I'm worried he got too much of the Ativan I ground up and mixed in with the Cheval Blanc. I didn't know exactly how much to put in because I didn't know how much he would drink, so I added enough that even a glass would be enough to knock him out. It turns out he drank the whole thing.

I rise from my desk and stand over him. His almost too handsome features are slack, with a little drool in the corner of his mouth, and his sun-streaked hair is gelled within an inch of its life. I have a pair of scissors in my desk drawer, and for a moment, I am seized with the almost irrepressible urge to take them out and plunge them into his chest. That would end the blackmail once and for all. Of course, that would be unbelievably stupid. I'm sure the police would find out that he came here for an appointment and never left. I'd rather not go to jail for murder. It doesn't matter that the victim really and truly deserved it. That the world would be a better place without him.

Instead, I reach for my phone and send off a text:

Come downstairs.

I walk around the side of the desk. EJ's phone is jutting out of his pocket. I slide it out gently, although he's sleeping so soundly I doubt I could wake him up if I wanted to. He has an iPhone that's a slightly newer model than mine. I pick up his right hand and press his thumb on the home button. It reads his fingerprint and the screen instantly unlocks. I release his hand, and his arm drops limply back onto the sofa.

I go into his photos. He doesn't have many of them. I get the feeling that EJ is a bit of a loner—he hardly ever mentions his friends. Mostly, there are a few photos of him standing in front of a mirror with his shirt off. And a few more where he's flexing his muscles. Then a few more of him completely naked. I scroll through those quickly. After the naked pictures, there are some of me. These were taken without my permission. There's one of me coming out of my house. Climbing into my car. And then one fuzzy one of what appears to be my bedroom window. Thank God, the blinds are mostly shut and you can't see much.

Once I get rid of this stupid video, this man is never coming on my property again. I'll get a restraining order if I have to.

Finally, I find what I'm looking for. The video from the parking lot. I watch it one more time, the bile rising in my throat. I had hoped it wasn't as bad as I had thought, but it is. It's just as bad. I seem so suspicious as my eyes dart around to make sure nobody's watching me, then I slash that tire. The expression on my face is almost demonic.

I nearly jump out of my skin when I hear the knock on my office door. I pull it up open gently—Luke is standing there, a deep crease between his eyebrows.

'Okay,' he says. 'I'm here.'

I hold out the phone to him. 'This is the video. I want you to eliminate any traces of it off this phone.'

He takes the phone from me, although he's unable to wipe the disapproving look from his eyes. His index finger hovers over the screen, and I grab his arm.

'Don't watch the video,' I say.

'I wasn't going to.'

I purse my lips. 'You looked like you were going to press Play.'

He lets out a huff. 'I can't delete this video from the phone if you won't let me touch the screen, Adrienne.'

Fine. I respectfully take a step back and allow him to do his thing with the phone. While he's working on it, I go back into the office, where EJ is still lying slumped on my leather sofa. I frown down at him, trying to make out the rise and fall of his chest. He is very, very still.

Christ, I didn't kill him, did I?

Very gently, I place my fingers on his left wrist, over his radial artery. I hold my breath, feeling around for his pulse.

I don't feel anything. Oh no.

Just before I can start panicking, he lets out a shudder

and shifts his position on the couch, pulling his arm out of my grasp. Thank God, he's alive. But I'm definitely going to have to help him get home.

I reach into his pocket gently and pull out his keys. He's got the key fob on the ring for his Porsche, then a couple of other keys. I do not know which one opens his front door, but there aren't that many. Luke can figure that out when he gets there.

When I come out of the office, Luke is standing there, his arms at his sides, EJ's phone in his right hand. 'It's done,' he says.

'And you didn't watch the video?'

'No.'

'You swear.'

'I swear.'

He hands me the phone, and I lay the house keys in his palm. He sucks in a breath when he sees them.

'Adrienne,' he says quietly, 'I really don't want to do this.'

Not this again. I assumed when he showed up here, he was done protesting. 'It's not that big a deal.'

'It *is* a big deal.' His eyes are wide behind his glasses. 'We drugged him, and now we're breaking into his house and hacking into his computer. That's a really big deal.'

There's a famous experiment by a Yale psychologist named Stanley Milgram—or should I say, *infamous*. The experiment measured the willingness of study participants to perform terrible acts when instructed to do so by an authority figure. Subjects were led to believe they were participating in an experiment in which they were a 'teacher' administering electric shocks to another subject—the 'learner'—every time he got the answer to a question wrong.

In reality, the 'learner' was an actor. And the electric shocks were fake.

During the experiment, the learner would beg for mercy. He would plead for the experiment to stop. He would complain about a heart condition. But the experimenter overseeing the study would tell the subject to keep administering the shocks of increasing intensity. The subjects grew increasingly uncomfortable as the experiment proceeded, but here is the amazing part:

Every single subject administered shocks of at least 300 V. And more than half of them administered a shock of 450 V—a fatal shock if it had been real.

The purpose of the experiment was to explain the psychology of genocide. That the Nazis did terrible things just because they were told to do so. But I have a different interpretation.

I believe that any human being is capable of terrible things if you push them hard enough.

So is Luke.

'Please do this for me, Luke.' My eyes fill with tears—I'm not sure if they're real or not. 'You're the only one who can help me. He's a terrible person. He's going to destroy me if I don't get this video off his computer.'

He shakes his head. 'Whatever is on that video … maybe you should just deal with it.'

'I *can't*.'

'Well, I don't think I can do this.'

I take a step back. 'So that's it. You're going to let this man destroy my entire life when you have a chance to stop him.'

'Adrienne . . .'

The tears are running down my cheeks now. 'You don't trust me. Even after all this time.'

'I trust you.'

'Then why won't you help me?'

Luke stares down at the set of keys in his hand. He exhales slowly. 'Okay. I'll do my best. But no promises.'

'Thank you, Luke.'

I throw my arms around him in an uncharacteristically affectionate gesture. Usually, he's the affectionate one. But this time, he just stands there stiffly under my embrace.

Luke plugs the address I gave him for EJ's house into his GPS, and then he takes off, with a promise to text me when he's on his way back. I don't know what I'm going to do if he says he can't get into that computer. As of now, I don't have a plan B. But I believe in Luke. He can do this.

It's been well over an hour since Luke left.

I've been babysitting EJ this whole time while he sleeps on my sofa. When he gets too quiet, I come over to make sure he is still breathing. He's fine though. I had been concerned about him waking up too soon, but I'm not worried about that any more. He's really conked out. My biggest concern right now is how I'm going to get him home. Luke is not going to be thrilled about helping me, but I don't think I can do it on my own.

Luke. What's taking him so long?

I chew on my thumbnail as I contemplate things that could have gone wrong. Maybe Luke couldn't get into the computer, which is undoubtedly password protected. Maybe a neighbour saw him entering the house and called the cops. Or possibly most likely, he decided not to go through with it after all and I'm never going to see him again.

Then my phone buzzes. Luke's name flashes on the screen.

I scoop it up and press the green button. 'Hello? Luke?'

'It's done.'

All the anxiety drains out of my body, and I feel like I'm going to pass out. 'Really? You deleted it from his computer?'

'Yes.'

'Oh my God,' I breathe. 'Thank you. Thank you so much. Was ... was it difficult?'

There's a long silence on the other end of the line. 'I don't want to talk about it.'

'Okay.' I clear my throat. 'You're coming back to my house?'

His voice is a monotone. 'Yes.'

'Okay.' I squeeze the phone until my fingers tingle. 'Thank you for doing this, Luke.'

'Yeah.'

'I ... I love you.'

'I'll see you later,' he says. And he hangs up on me.

I lower the phone and stare at the blank screen, a sick feeling in my stomach. Luke is pissed off at me. He's lost respect for me. I'm not sure if he watched the video or not, but I don't know if it matters. He's angry that I made him do this. I did this to get EJ out of my life. But I may have inad vertently eliminated Luke from my life as well.

My eyes fill with very real tears. I don't want to lose Luke. I'm not sorry I asked him to do this, because I didn't have a choice. I don't want to stop seeing him. I don't want him to empty the drawer I gave him in my bedroom. I want to give him *more* drawers.

I want him to move in with me. I've never felt this way before, but I realize it now. I want him here every night. For the rest of my life.

I can't lose him over this. I *can't*.

CHAPTER 35

TRICIA

PRESENT DAY

The final EJ tape comes to a close. Soon after lunch, I retrieved the rest of the EJ tapes from the hidden room, and now I've finished all of them. This last tape is labelled in black, not red like all the other final sessions, but there are no other tapes after this one. And it only goes on for about twenty minutes.

The strangest thing about it is how EJ sounds toward the end of the tape. His voice is almost slurred, but Dr Hale doesn't seem the slightest bit concerned. She's a doctor, for God's sake. Shouldn't she be worried that her patient is slurring his speech?

EJ did mention drinking some wine. But if he's anything like Ethan, even a bottle of wine isn't enough to get him to slur his speech.

It's strange.

Now that I have finished the stack of EJ tapes, I decide to take a break. I've been listening to tapes in here the entire afternoon, and the sun has now dropped in the sky. It looks like we are definitely going to be spending another night here.

I don't know what to tell Ethan. He wants to buy this house, but I just can't imagine it. I love him, but not enough to live *here*.

I slide off my gold wedding band, remembering the first time Ethan slipped it onto my finger. Years ago, before I knew Ethan, I had been engaged to another man, and we had been planning a giant wedding, but it ended up not working out. This time, all I wanted was a small, perfect ceremony. It was so intimate, and for a moment, while our eyes locked together at the altar, it was like the two of us were the only people in the world.

Ethan and I are meant for each other. I know it. I want to give him everything he wants, but I don't know if I can give him this. This *house*.

I tilt the ring a bit so I can read the inscription. Ethan + Tricia Forever. I love that inscription ... I read it some times to comfort me. I believe it with all my heart. Ethan and I are made for each other, and we will be together forever. Till death do us part.

A noise from outside the office startles me, and the ring slips from my fingers. Unfortunately, it lands on its side and starts to roll. It rolls all the way across the desk, onto the floor, and before I can stop it, it has rolled under the leather sofa.

Great. Just my luck.

I get down on my knees and elbows on the floor. The base of the sofa is low to the floor, with less than an inch of space between them. It's also pushed up against the wall. I squint underneath, but everything is dark. I can't even tell where my ring might have gone under there.

My purse is on the desk, so I grab my phone from inside and turn on the flashlight function. I can see a bit, but mostly dust bunnies. I don't see any sign of a ring reflecting the light from my phone.

Damn it.

I try to reach underneath the couch, but there isn't enough space down there. I can get my hand underneath about to my wrist, and then it will go no farther.

I straighten up, realizing too late that I should have taken the white cashmere sweater off before getting down on my elbows. I do my best to brush off the dust, then I consider my options.

There's no way I'm going to reach that ring without moving the couch. I could attempt to move it on my own, but I don't know if it's a good idea while I'm pregnant. I've heard you're not supposed to do a lot of heavy lifting.

That leaves one option. I have to get Ethan to help me move it.

He's probably still upstairs working. Or the sound that startled me was him coming down for dinner. Either way, he'll be happy to help me with the couch. He loves doing stuff like that. Damsel in distress, etc.

When I come out of Dr Hale's office, the first floor is silent. Ethan isn't down here. I don't hear anyone down here. He must still be working upstairs.

And then I hear a creaking sound from upstairs. And then something that almost sounds like a door slamming shut.

That must've been Ethan. I already know he's working up there. He probably went to the bathroom or something. There's no reason to worry.

I mount the spiral staircase, irritated that the hall light is off upstairs. There are too many light switches in this house. Of course, Ethan would argue that's something easy to fix. We could put in a switch downstairs that could control the upstairs hall light. Or we could have a sensor that would turn it on automatically as we walk up the stairs.

When I get to the top of the steps, the first thing I do is flick on the light. I breathe a sigh of relief as the hallway fills with light, albeit dim. I hate this house when it's dark. I feel so much better when the lights are on.

Until I notice that the pull cord for the attic, hanging from the ceiling, is swaying. Like the trapdoor to the attic was recently in motion.

It could be the wind. But it's not that windy inside the house. And even if there were a slight breeze, it's still swinging quite a bit.

I can't think about that right now though. I'll tell Ethan about the ring, we'll get it back, and then I'll have him check out the attic. It's not negotiable. I'm not moving into this house unless he checks up there.

I knock on the door to the room Ethan is using, my hand feeling oddly naked without my wedding band. I've only had it for six months, but it's become a part of me. I already miss it.

'Come in!' he calls out.

I crack open the door and find Ethan at the desk again, sitting at his computer in the same position I found him earlier. It's like he hasn't budged an inch.

'Hungry?' he asks.

'Actually,' I say, 'I need your help.' He arches an eyebrow. 'Oh?'

I hold up my left hand. 'My wedding band rolled under the sofa. I need you to move it so I can get it back.' He tilts his head to the side. 'Why did you take it off in the first place? Are you pretending to be single?'

I snort. 'No. I was just looking at the inscription.'

A smile spreads across his lips. 'Ethan and Tricia forever.'

'Right.'

Ethan stretches as he stands up from his chair so that I catch a glimpse of the golden hair on his belly. He slams the cover of his laptop closed but leaves it there. He's obviously planning to do more work later. He's thrown his all into this startup company. He had one in the past that didn't do well, but this one is quite the budding success.

'By the way,' I say, 'right before I came in here, were you by any chance in another room? Maybe the bathroom?'

Please say yes. Please.

He frowns. 'No, I've been sitting here working for at least the last hour.'

Of course. I'm not even the tiniest bit surprised.

He follows me down the stairs to Dr Hale's office. My breath catches for a moment as I try to remember if I put the tapes back in the drawer before leaving the office. I'm relieved when we get into the office and find that I remembered to stash them out of sight. I can't imagine Ethan's reaction if he found out what I've been doing here.

He looks down at the couch and folds his arms. 'This is where you lost it?'

I nod. 'Pretty sure. I saw it roll under there.'

'All right then.'

He leans over and grabs the edge of the couch. I guess it's not as heavy as I thought it was, because he easily heaves it out of the way. Almost immediately, I spot the tiny circle of gold on the floor.

'There it is!' I cry.

I bend down to pick up the ring, but when I'm close to the floor, I realize there's something else down there. It's some sort of handle. Why is there a handle on the floor?

Instinctively, I tap the heel of my bare foot against the wooden planks. That's when I realize it.

The floor is hollow.

'What's wrong?' Ethan asks.

I scoop my ring off the ground and quickly secure it on my finger. When I straighten up, I tap on the floor again with my foot. 'There's some kind of compartment or something down here. It's hollow.'

'Really?'

Ethan joins me and taps on the floor with his foot.

There's no mistaking the sound.

'There's something down here,' I say, staring at the wooden planks.

'I think you're right.'

Ethan grabs the sofa again and shifts it to the other side of the room. Now that it's out of the way, I can see the full rectangular outline on the floor. It's some sort of large compartment under the floor.

What could be down there? More tapes? I suppose that's a possibility, but I have a feeling that's not it. I also have a feeling that we are the first people to discover this hidden compartment since Dr Hale lived here.

'What do you think?' Ethan grins at me. 'Hidden treasure?'

'I don't know ...'

'Well,' he says. 'Let's open it up and see.'

He bends down to grab the handle, but before he can, I seize his arm. 'Maybe we shouldn't. Maybe we should tell the police and let them check it out.'

'Are you kidding me? You really don't want to look? Who *are* you, and what have you done with my wife?'

I grimace. 'I'm sorry. I just ... I don't know if it's a crime scene or something. We don't want to disturb it. Like, what if there are fingerprints we need to preserve?'

'Nah. It's probably just where the doctor stashed her jewelry or something.' He winks at me. 'You could have your pick of it.'

Does he honestly think I would ever touch her jewelry? I wouldn't. I'm sorry I took her sweater even though I was cold. It's burning my skin.

'It's not a big deal.' He shrugs. 'Let's just open it.' 'No, please—'

But Ethan isn't listening to me. He reaches down, grabs the handle, and hauls open the lid to the hidden compartment.

And when I see what's inside, my heart drops.

CHAPTER 36

ADRIENNE

BEFORE

When Luke returns with the keys, I'm already waiting at the front door. I fling it open before he even has a chance to knock. He blinks in surprise, his hand frozen in the air.

'Hello,' I say.

For the first time, I realize he has not shaved today. He's got that stubble on his chin that he always used to have when he worked at the clinic. Once we started dating, he began shaving daily, because he knows I prefer it.

'Hey.' He shoves his hand into his pocket and fishes out the keys. He drops them in my hand like they're made of something dirty. 'Here.'

'Thank you again.'

'Uh-huh.'

'You, uh ...' I scratch my neck. 'You got everything off the computer?'

'I said I did, didn't I?' There's an edge to his voice that's unfamiliar. He's always so kind and even-tempered, it's hard to hear him talk to me this way. 'But like I told you, I can't be sure there aren't other copies somewhere else in his house.'

'Did you look around?'

'*No.*' He glares at me. 'I didn't.'

'Oh.' I cough. 'And, um, you didn't ... watch the video, right?'

'No, I watched it.'

My face burns. 'Luke, you promised you wouldn't!'

'Well, it's too late. I watched it.' He frowns. 'I had to find out what was so bad that you were willing to go to so much trouble to get rid of it.'

I hang my head. 'I didn't want you to see.'

'What the hell were you doing?' His usually mild brown eyes are flashing. 'You slashed some guy's tires? Why would you do that?'

'I was having a bad day.' I avert my eyes, unable to look at him. It doesn't matter any more what I say. I've lost him. 'Hasn't that ever happened to you? You had a bad day and did something stupid?'

'I never slashed anyone's tires.'

'Well, maybe you're better than me then.'

He's quiet for a moment, looking down at his sneakers. Finally, he says, 'What did the guy in the Jetta do to you anyway?'

'He stole my parking spot. And I was in a rush to get to the clinic on time.'

His lips part and he just stares at me for a second. 'Are you *kidding* me?'

I shake my head slowly. 'I had a patient scheduled. I didn't want to be late.'

It all sounds ridiculously inadequate when I say it out loud.

'Jesus.' He cracks his knuckles. 'You are really something. All that over a stolen parking spot. You're unbelievable.'

I'm scared to say anything else. Usually, I'm extremely skilled at knowing what to say to make somebody else feel better. It's my job after all. But it's never meant quite this much. I try to keep my mouth shut, but I can't help myself. I finally blurt out, 'Do you hate me now?'

His eyebrows shoot up. 'Hate you?'

'Well ...' I squeeze my sweaty hands together. 'You seem like you're angry with me. And you're barely looking at me.'

'Yeah.' He sighs. 'I'm not going to lie—I'm not thrilled with you right now. But I see why you wanted to get rid of that video. And ... I'm glad I could help you.' A lopsided smile creeps onto his face. 'Also, it's good to know that you're not so perfect either.'

I return an equally crooked smile. 'I never claimed I was.'

'Okay, now that we've settled that ...' Luke's eyes flicker in the direction of my office. 'Let's get this asshole back to his car.'

I'm in an incredibly good mood as I make the drive back from EJ's house in my Lexus with Luke in the passenger seat. About an hour ago, he assisted me in loading EJ into the passenger's seat of his Porsche. He insisted on being the one to drive the car with EJ inside, because he didn't want me in there in case EJ woke up during the half-hour drive. Although part of me feels like he just wanted an excuse to drive a Porsche.

When we reached EJ's house (paid for by his parents), Luke parked the Porsche in the driveway. He left EJ passed out in the passenger seat, then he got into my car, and now we're on our way home.

I have the music on in the car—an opera I went to recently in the city—the window is down, and the air feels wonderful on my face. For four months, EJ had been holding that horrible video over my head and using it to manipulate me. Now I've taken care of the problem. All thanks to Luke.

If the opera were in English and I knew the words, I would sing along.

Luke is strapped into the passenger seat, absently staring out the side window. He did absolutely everything I asked of him, and although he wasn't thrilled about it, he fixed my problem. As I study his profile at a red light, I feel a rush of affection.

'I love you,' I say again.

He turns away from the window. I reach out my hand, and he takes it. The squeeze he gives me is half-hearted, but I can't entirely blame him after the day we've had. 'I love you too.'

'And maybe,' I say, 'we can look into you moving in? Like, soon.'

His eyes widen. 'Really?'

Butterflies flutter in my stomach. 'Really.'

For the first time since I talked him into doing this, I coax a genuine smile out of him. 'Okay,' he says.

I turn down the tiny road that leads to my house. The road is paved, but just barely. I always loved the solitude of my isolated kingdom, but I'm ready to share that kingdom. After all, what's the point of six bedrooms if you're only using one of them?

As I park the car, my phone buzzes in my pocket. A text message. Ever since EJ started blackmailing me, the buzz of a text message used to fill me with dread. But now I am strangely calm as I remove my phone from my pocket and look down at the screen.

You bitch. You broke into my house.

Technically, the statement is not accurate on two counts. First of all, it was Luke who entered his house. Not me. Second, we did not break in since we had a copy of his keys. But EJ would not appreciate me pointing these things out, even though I'm tempted to do so.

A second message appears on the screen:

I'm going to kill you.

'What's wrong?' Luke asks me. He's gotten out of the car, but I'm still in the driver's seat. He's peering through the open window at me.

EJ does not intend to kill me. He's angry because I got the better of him for a change. If he really wanted to kill me, he would keep his mouth shut. You don't send somebody a text message expressing your intention to commit a crime if you're genuinely planning to 3do it.

But if I show this message to Luke, he won't see it that way. It will surely worry him and make him think we have made a terrible mistake. He doesn't understand men like EJ. I do.

'Nothing,' I say. 'Nothing is wrong.'

I click on EJ's number and block it on my phone. Then I get out of the car and follow Luke into the house.

CHAPTER 37

TRICIA

PRESENT DAY

I'm going to throw up.

I clamp a hand over my mouth, but it's unstoppable. I shove Ethan aside and make a mad dash for the kitchen, just in time to hurl into the sink. I grip the edges of the kitchen counter, my vision blurring.

'Tricia?'

Ethan's hand touches my back, and I shudder at his touch, and not in a good way. I close my eyes, trying to block out what I just saw in the compartment under the floorboards. But I can't. I'll be seeing that image until the day I die.

I'm sorry we came here. Sorry we got started on any of this.

'I guess we know what happened to Dr Hale now,' Ethan says in a husky voice.

'I guess so,' I choke out.

I didn't know what to expect when Ethan opened up that compartment. But that was like nothing I'd ever seen before. A rotting corpse, stuffed under the floorboards. I don't know how long it takes for a human to turn into nothing but bones after death, but this body hadn't reached that stage yet. There was still dried-out black skin clinging to the bones.

And scraps of clothing. What possibly used to be a blue shirt. Denim pants. Evidence that once upon a time, that desiccated corpse was a real person. They put on pants and a shirt that morning, never suspecting how their day would end.

'I need some air,' I gasp.

Before Ethan can protest, I push past him and stumble toward the front door. It takes me a second to fumble with the locks, but when I finally get it open, I almost cry with relief. I step out onto the front porch, my socks sinking into the snow that accumulated there last night.

Now that the sun is down, the temperature is definitely below freezing. And all I'm wearing is a pair of blue jeans, a flimsy blouse, that white cashmere sweater, and my socks. By all rights, I should be freezing my ass off. But it feels good. It gives me a distraction from the horrible image I will never get out of my head.

'Christ, Tricia, it's freezing out here!'

Naturally, Ethan has followed me out to the front porch. At least he was smart enough to put on his boots and tug on his coat. He's also holding my coat.

'Put this on,' he orders me.

I let him lace my arms into the coat, although it probably feels to him like he's dressing a rag doll. He throws an arm around my shoulders, but I shrug him off. I don't want him to touch me right now.

'You should put on shoes,' he says quietly. 'You're going to get frostbite.'

I stare off into the distance. Snow as far as I can see. How are we ever going to get out of here? And we're stuck here, *with a dead body*.

'Tricia? Are you okay?'

'*No*.'

Ethan grimaces. 'I'm so sorry you had to see that. I never should have opened the compartment.'

'I've never seen a dead body before.' I glance over at him. 'Have you?'

He hesitates a second too long. 'No.'

'*Have* you?'

'Well …' He shoves his hands into his coat pockets. 'At funerals, obviously sometimes there's an open casket. So …'

I swallow. 'We really have to spend the night here?'

Ethan stares off into the distance. 'I guess I could go back down the road on foot. See if I could flag down a car and call for a truck to plow us out.'

'And leave me alone with that dead body?'

He sighs. 'We don't have a lot of options. I still think we should wait for the morning. At the very least, it won't be so cold.'

At his words, I realize that my feet have gone completely numb. I really am going to get frostbite if I stand here much longer. 'Let's go back inside.'

'That's a good idea.'

Ethan puts his hand on the small of my back and leads me gently back into the house, even though a wave of nausea hits me as I step into the living room. My socks are completely soaked from the snow, and I still can't feel my feet. Ethan leads me to the sofa and gently sits me down.

'You need to warm up,' he says firmly.

'Yeah,' I mumble.

I can't seem to stop shaking. I shiver almost violently as he tugs off my frigid socks. My feet have turned an angry red colour. Ethan clucks his tongue. 'I'm going to get a bowl of warm water.'

He's so calm about the whole thing. How can he be so calm? What we saw in that compartment was one of the most horrifying things I've ever seen in my life. It was like something out of a horror movie. Yet Ethan doesn't seem at all upset about it. Shouldn't he be *upset*?

But at the same time, I'm grateful he's so calm. He's such a great husband, and he's going to be a great father. You need somebody like that—somebody who is so levelheaded in a time of crisis. That's Ethan.

I close my eyes, listening to the sound of water running in the kitchen. I take a deep breath, trying to control my shaking. I hear footsteps, and when I open my eyes again, Ethan is standing in front of me, holding a large glass bowl filled with water.

'Put your feet in,' he instructs me.

I oblige. The sensation is slowly returning to my toes, and it feels almost like they're burning as I submerge them in the lukewarm liquid. Somehow it calms me down though. The shaking is easing up just a bit.

'Better?' he asks.

I nod wordlessly.

Ethan drops down beside me on the sofa. He puts his arm around my shoulders, and this time I let him. I rest my head against him as the tremors in my body gradually subside. Before I can completely calm down, something makes my head jerk up.

It's a crash. Coming from Dr Hale's office. Ethan hears it too. He sits up, his whole body rigid. He's been denying it the whole time we've been here, saying that I'm imagining things, but now he knows I'm right. There's somebody else in this house. There is somebody in Dr Hale's office.

That or the corpse has come back to life.

CHAPTER 38

ADRIENNE

BEFORE

Luke and I are grocery shopping together.

Grocery stores are an exercise in psychological manipulation. It is virtually impossible to enter a supermarket intending to buy a quart of milk and emerge with only the milk. First, consider the entrance. Once you enter the grocery store, you must traverse the entire store in order to reach the checkout line.

And where do the entrances to grocery stores usually leave you? In the produce department. You are surrounded by scents, textures, and bright colours that result in a surge of endorphins. The lighting of the store is manipulated to make fruits and vegetables appear at their brightest and best. And of course, the dairy aisle—one of the most popular locations to visit—is always hidden in the back of the store so you are forced to pass through a wealth of tempting products before reaching it.

Even the way the shelves are organized is a psychological trap. The most expensive items are always placed conveniently at adult eye level, with the generic brands placed down by your knees. Sugary cereals or other items meant to appeal to children are placed at eye level for children. Even the giant size of the shopping carts is intended to encourage more purchases.

'Even the music is meant to manipulate us,' I explain to Luke. 'A study of supermarket shoppers found people spend more time shopping when stores play music. You'll notice there are no windows or clocks or skylights that give you any external time cues.'

'That's fascinating,' Luke says as he throws a box of corn flakes into our cart. 'I never realized how twisted supermarkets are.'

'So the key is not to be fooled by their subtle tactics.' I seize the handle of the cart and navigate us away from the bright boxes of the cereal aisle. 'We have a grocery shopping list. We need to stick to exactly what is on the list. No impulse purchases.'

He grins at me. 'You are so wise.'

'I'm serious. The more time we linger in the supermarket, the more unnecessary items we will purchase.'

He nods thoughtfully. 'So ... would this be a big no-no then?'

With those words, he grabs me and his lips find mine. Right in the middle of the supermarket. And despite my determination not to dawdle here, I don't mind one bit.

In the week since we deleted the video from EJ's phone and home computer, Luke and I have grown closer than ever. He was anxious about EJ retaliating, so he insisted on spending the next few nights at my house. But EJ didn't try to contact me—I've blocked him on my phone, and he never showed up at my front door like I worried he might.

Even after those first few days though, Luke hasn't gone home. Well, just once to grab more clothing, but then he came back right away.

As I allow Luke to kiss me right in the middle of aisle six at the grocery store, I realize that this is the happiest I have ever been. I have a wonderful man in my life, my book is coming out soon, and I have defused the EJ situation. And I have this feeling that more good things are soon to come.

'Dr Hale!'

I jerk away from Luke, guilty for my display of affection in a public place. It was utterly unprofessional. Although Luke doesn't seem the slightest bit sorry. He has a dopey grin on his face.

When I turn around, I recognize one of my patients. GW. The woman who was first convinced that her mailman was trying to kill her, then her pharmacist, and more recently her son. When I'm alone with patients in my office and I hear their darkest thoughts, sometimes I wonder how they manage to function in their lives. But here is Gail, looking very put together in a fetching pink sweater and khaki slacks, with her makeup more perfectly applied than mine after Luke smudged my lipstick with that kiss. I wonder if she's been taking her medications.

'Hello, Gail.' I wipe my lips self-consciously, ignoring the burning sensation on my face. 'It's nice seeing you.'

'Oh dear," Gail murmurs. 'I didn't mean to interrupt you and your gentleman friend. I just got excited when I saw you.'

'That's quite all right.' I tug at the collar of my blouse and glance at Luke, who is looking at me expectantly. 'Luke, this is Gail, a patient of mine. Gail, this is Luke. My, um, friend.'

Luke smirks at the description of 'friend' and Gail seems amused as well. But as I got into my thirties, the term boyfriend felt strange on my lips. After all, Luke is hardly a *boy*.

'I haven't seen you for a bit, Gail,' I say, attempting to alleviate the awkwardness. 'Is everything all right?'

'Everything is great!' Her jowls jiggle as she smiles. 'I took your advice and sat down with my son, and we had a wonderful talk. It made me realize how right you were about the stupid paranoid thoughts I was having about everyone. It completely turned things around.' She beams at me. 'You really helped me.'

She *looks* much better. She sometimes used to show up at our appointments slightly disheveled, with the scent of alcohol emanating from her—a fact that I gently tried to bring up a few times, and she always laughed it off and changed the subject. But today, she just smells like perfume. Lilacs, I think.

'I'm so glad you're doing well.' My phone buzzes inside my purse. A text message. 'It was my pleasure.'

Gail turns her attention to Luke. 'Your friend here is a wonderful doctor. She has *such* a brilliant mind.'

He grins at me. 'I know it'

While Gail goes on and on, extolling my virtues,

I rifle around in my handbag to retrieve my phone, to make sure I'm not being texted about any emergencies regarding my patients. I glance down at the screen and see a message from an unfamiliar number.

It's a video.

I don't need to click on it to know what it is. I recognize my own image right alongside that red Jetta. I have seen this video so many times, I see it in my sleep. But I had thought it was gone forever.

I sent Luke to get rid of that video on EJ's computer. But it seems like he had another copy tucked away somewhere.

I glance up at Luke and Gail, who are still talking. I type into my phone with trembling fingers:

What do you want?

I stare at the screen, waiting for his response. Three bubbles appear, and I imagine his finger tapping out letters on his phone. Finally, two words appear on the screen:

Talk tonight.

I have just made things so much worse.

CHAPTER 39

ADRIENNE

After we unpack the groceries, I send Luke back to his apartment, feigning a headache. I don't tell him about the video. If I do, he'll be furious with me. He didn't want to do it in the first place, and he warned me there could be other copies floating around.

And I definitely don't want him to know that EJ wants to meet me tonight. He would want to be there. And even though on some level, I desperately want him to be there, this is my mess. I need to figure it out on my own.

My plan is to offer him money. A *lot* of money. I have come up with a sum that I believe will be sufficient to get him to leave me alone, and I'm willing to go as high as twice that amount if I must. Or even higher if I can somehow guarantee he will be out of my life for good.

My refrigerator is filled with food, but I have no appetite. Ironically, all I can stomach for dinner is a few of the saltines I ate that first night Luke came to help me set up the security system. And even those churn around in my belly.

It isn't until past nine that the doorbell rings.

The chimes echo throughout the house. I've been sitting on the sectional sofa, chewing off the better part of my fingernails, and at the sound of those chimes, I want to regurgitate all the saltines I ate. Suddenly, I wish I had asked Luke to stay. I don't want to do this alone.

But I have no choice. EJ isn't going away. Not until he gets what he wants.

I open the camera app on my phone, and I see him standing there. His blonde hair is gleaming in the porch lights, and his hands are shoved into his pockets. I try to read his expression, but the camera angle is wrong. I take a deep breath and force myself to stand up. I walk over to the door, wiping my sweaty hands on my slacks.

I undo the locks slowly. I crack open the door, and there he is, standing on my front porch, a big grin splitting his face. I am seized with the sudden urge to scratch his eyes out until there's nothing left but two hollow sockets. I ball my right hand into a fist.

'Aren't you going to ask me to come in, Doc?'

I step aside, allowing the door to swing open. He steps into my house, and my stomach sinks. I thought I'd never have to see him again. I had been counting on it.

'You don't look so good, Doc,' he says. 'You coming down with a cold or something?'

'What do you want from me?' I hiss at him.

He throws back his head and laughs. 'You're acting like you don't like me very much.'

Like all narcissists, EJ can be incredibly charming when he wants to be. Most people like him when they first meet him, but they all eventually see through his act.

I disliked him immediately. I only continued our sessions because his mother begged me. Now I regret it.

'Let's get this over with.' I fold my arms across my chest, trying not to let on how much I'm shaking. 'I'll write you a cheque right now. How much do you want?'

'Oh, I'm not concerned about money any more.' He waves a hand. 'I'm not sure if you heard, but my parents were in a terrible car wreck last month. They didn't survive.' He pulls an exaggerated sad face. 'And I'm their only heir, so … you know.'

I hug my chest. It's exactly what he described to me when he was imagining his parents' death. *My mother is a terrible driver. One of these days, she'll be driving with my father in the car, and she'll just drive right into a Mack truck and they'll both be killed.* And now it's happened.

Even though I never liked EJ, I always thought he was harmless. I am ashamed that even as a psychiatrist, I completely misdiagnosed him, which may have been the most costly mistake I have made in my career. But now I know the truth.

The man is a psychopath.

'What do you want?' I croak.

The smile playing on EJ's lips makes me want to smack him. 'Oh, I've been thinking long and hard about that one, Dr Hale.'

I swallow. 'I'll give you another prescription for oxycodone. One more.'

He snorts. 'Sorry, Doc. That's not going to do it any more. Not after the shit you pulled.'

'Just tell me what you want.'

'What do I want?' He takes a step toward me, and I back away, still hugging my chest. 'I want *you*, Adrienne.'

I feel dizzy. 'You mean more sessions?'

'Call it whatever you want.' He takes another step toward me, that smile still stretching his lips grotesquely. 'I want you to strip down naked and let me do anything I want to do to you. *Anything*.'

My knees wobble. 'No. Out of the question.'

'Don't rule it out so quickly.' He reaches out to touch me, and I jerk away. 'You might enjoy it—I sure will. I bet you're getting tired of that nerdy boyfriend of yours. I bet he's terrible in bed.'

'Get out of my house,' I snarl at him. 'Get out or I'm calling the police.'

He arches an eyebrow. 'Are you sure you want to do that?'

'Yes.' I stick out my chin. 'If you feel you have to destroy me with that video, go ahead. I'm not going along with this any more. I won't play your games.'

'Oh, Adrienne,' he sighs. 'Unfortunately, it's not just about you any more.'

He fishes his phone out of his pocket. I stare at him while he jabs at the screen. After a second, he holds out his phone to me. I shake my head.

'Take it.' He thrusts the phone into my chest. 'You're going to want to see this. I promise.'

Oh God. What is going on?

My hands are trembling so much that I almost drop the phone. I stare down at the screen, where a video is playing. But this isn't a video of me in the parking lot. It's a different video.

It's an image of the outside of EJ's house. After a second, a familiar figure comes into view. It's Luke. He digs into his pocket, pulls out the keys, and unlocks the front door. The video then cuts to the inside of the house. Luke—searching through the rooms, looking for the laptop computer. Using a letter opener to jimmy open the lock on a desk drawer, then pulling out the laptop. Sitting down at the laptop to start the process of breaking into EJ's computer.

It's all there on video.

'This wouldn't be too good for your boyfriend's career, would it?'

I'm going to be sick. I lean forward and retch, but there's not enough in my stomach. EJ watches in amusement, then bursts out laughing. 'Boy, you're really not too excited about hooking up with me, are you?'

'Please don't do this to him,' I gasp.

'It's your own fault. You're the one who dragged him into it.' He shakes his head. 'This is what I really wanted all along. From the moment I first walked into your office and saw you in that sexy little dress suit, looking so uptight with your hair pinned back. Acting like you knew it all, more than anyone else—more than me anyway. And I always had a thing for redheads.' He looks pointedly at the phone still in my hand. 'But that first video wasn't enough. I knew you wouldn't go for it. Not unless I had something bigger. So … thanks for that.'

'Please,' I whisper. 'I'll give you anything else. Pills, money ...'

'I've got a guy to get me pills now.' He plucks his phone out of my hand. 'All I want is you.'

I just shake my head.

'Tell you what.' He shoves his phone back into his pocket. 'Why don't you think about it for a few days? Think about whether avoiding one night of pleasure with me is worth destroying both of your lives.'

'I won't change my mind,' I whisper.

He tilts his head. 'I'm not so sure about that.'

With those words, he turns on his heels and walks out of my home. The door slams shut behind him, and it's only then that I sink onto the sofa, my entire body trembling.

What am I going to do?

CHAPTER 40

TRICIA

PRESENT DAY

'Don't move,' Ethan says.

He dashes into the kitchen, and I crane my neck just in time to see him pulling a knife from the knife block. He's searching for the biggest knife he can find, which turns out to be some sort of carving knife that looks about eight-inches long. It glints in the overhead light of the kitchen, and it looks pretty frightening from here. Then again, we don't know what the intruder is packing. If the intruder has a gun, the knife won't do us much good.

He told me not to move, but there's no way I'm sitting here on the couch while my husband possibly is shot to death. I tear my feet out of the bowl of warm water and sprint after him, leaving a trail of puddles behind me.

Ethan reaches the door to the office a second before I do. His eyes bulge at whatever he sees in the room, and his fingers whiten on the handle of the knife. 'Freeze,' I hear him say. 'Hands up!'

I stare into the office over his shoulder. Even though I expected it on some level, I'm shocked to see a man standing in the middle of the room, his trembling hands raised in the air. He has scraggly dark hair, badly in need of a haircut, and several weeks' growth of a beard on his face. He's wearing a pair of worn blue jeans and a sweatshirt with a hole in the sleeve. He sort of looks like a bum, except he's wearing eyeglasses, which seem oddly out of place.

'Who are you?' Ethan hisses.

'I …' The man's voice cracks like he hasn't spoken in a long time. 'I …'

'*Who are you?*'

'I just needed a place to stay for the night,' he says in a gruff voice. 'I don't have a place to live, and I … I didn't know anyone would be here.'

Ethan and the stranger regard each other with wary expressions on their faces. But I feel better. It's what I had suspected. A drifter is squatting in the house because he thought it was empty. And he doesn't seem to be armed or drunk or crazed. While he's taller than Ethan, he doesn't seem particularly muscular or scary—he's stick thin, like he hasn't had a decent meal in years.

But there's something about his voice. Something strangely familiar.

'I'm sorry.' The man clears some nasty-sounding phlegm from his throat. 'It was real cold out so I … Anyway, I'm sorry I busted in here. I … I'll go.'

For a moment, I feel a surge of sympathy. It can't be easy to be homeless in the middle of winter. Part of me wants to insist that he stay instead of casting him out into the cold. But another part of me feels like there's something fishy about his story.

Ethan looks like he's thinking the same thing. His grip on the carving knife hasn't eased up at all. 'What are you doing in this office then?'

He makes an excellent point. If this man were squatting here, why wouldn't he stay hidden? Why was he lurking around a place where he could easily be found? And then I notice how close he is to the opening to the compartment in the floor, which is now thankfully closed. It hits me what the crash we heard was.

It was the sound of the compartment slamming shut.

'I ... I wanted to see what all the commotion was about,' the man stammers.

Perhaps that could explain why he was in the office. But it doesn't explain why the portrait of Adrienne Hale materialized back on the wall in the middle of the night last night. Only one thing explains that.

'You're Luke,' I say. 'You're Adrienne Hale's boyfriend.'

CHAPTER 41

ADRIENNE

BEFORE

Luke has cooked us dinner tonight. It's chicken marsala. Slices of chicken breast braised in marsala wine sauce, butter, and garlic. It smells incredible, but I have not taken one bite. I have spent the last fifteen minutes pushing it around my plate, pretending to be eating even though I have no appetite.

'Is your chicken overcooked?' Luke cranes his neck to look at the little chunk that I sliced off. 'Mine is perfect, but yours was a little thinner. Is it too dry?'

'Not at all.' I force a smile. 'It's delicious. Really.' 'Then how come you've barely eaten a bite of it?' He frowns. 'Are you feeling sick? Is it a migraine?'

It has been two days since EJ told me what he wanted me to do. I wouldn't let Luke come over again last night, complaining that my head was still bothering me. But I couldn't put him off forever, so here he is.

I'm trying to put EJ out of my head, but I can't. All I

can think about is how EJ will destroy both of us if I don't do what he wants. But how can I? The thought of letting that man touch me makes me physically ill. Not to mention the fact that I can't even contemplate being with someone besides Luke. A few days ago, I had thought he might be the person I would spend the rest of my life with …

I have thought about nothing else besides my dilemma for the last two days. And I've concluded that there's only one solution to this problem.

I lay down my fork, push away my plate, and stare across the dining table at Luke. He pushes his glasses further up the bridge of his nose, a curious expression on his face. I fold my hands in front of me on the table.

'We have a problem,' I say.

He nods thoughtfully. 'You don't want me to move in.' God, is that what he thinks? 'Luke—'

'It's okay,' he says quickly. 'I know this is fast. I get it. I didn't want to push you. I mean, I'd love to live with you, but I'm okay if you want to wait.'

He's breaking my heart, because all I want is to live with this man. To spend my life with him. I have never felt this way before—never imagined I ever would—and it kills me that a vindictive monster is ruining the only relationship in my life that has ever mattered to me. 'Luke …' He reaches across the table and grabs one of my hands, pulling them apart. 'I have to tell you, Adrienne. After Darcy died, I honestly couldn't imagine ever falling for anyone else ever again. And then I met you, and … I just knew right away.' He squeezes my hand. 'Like I said, if you want to take it slower, that's fine. I'll wait as long as I have to.'

My eyes fill with tears. 'That's not it at all. I want you to move in too. But ...'

His brow creases. 'But what?'

'There's another copy of the video,' I blurt out.

For a second, it's so quiet you can hear the air conditioner whirring. Luke's jaw tightens as he absorbs this piece of information. 'What?'

'He must have had another copy saved somewhere.' I bite down on my lower lip. 'He sent it to me. And ... he's pretty pissed off.'

Luke snatches his hand away from mine, the affection disappearing from his face. 'Well, I told you that was a possibility. All we could do was get rid of the copies on his computer and his phone.'

That wasn't all Luke did. He told me he hadn't searched for any other copies, but he did. I could see him searching the desk drawers in that recording EJ showed me.

'Anyway,' I say, 'he's making demands again. Blackmailing me.' I can't bring myself to tell Luke what he wants. It's humiliating. Let him believe it's just money. 'It's never going to stop.'

He heaves a sigh. 'Yeah. I ... I don't know what to say. I don't think you should give in to him.'

'That video would destroy me.'

'*He's* destroying you. He's controlling your life. You can't let him do this to you.'

I suck in a breath. 'I know. You're right. He's going to hold this over me forever. As long as he's alive ...'

I let that last statement hang there. Luke's face clouds with confusion. 'What ... what are you saying, Adrienne?'

'I think you know.'

'Are you saying …?' He shakes his head. 'Look, you need to let him publish the video if he wants. Accept the consequences.'

'So I should let him wreck my life?'

'No … I mean, I don't think that video will wreck your life.' He shifts in his seat. 'You can spin it.'

'No. I can't.'

He grimaces. 'I don't know what to say. You don't have a choice. There's no alternative.'

'There's one other thing.' I square my shoulders, knowing that I've reached the moment of no return. 'He has another video.'

His long eyelashes flutter. 'Another …?'

'A video of you.'

'Of *me*?'

'He has a recording of you entering his house and breaking into his laptop.' The words come out in a rush. I want to get this over with. 'It even shows you breaking into his desk with a letter opener.'

The colour slowly drains out of Luke's face. 'Holy …'

'I'm so sorry, Luke.'

'*Sorry?*' The colour that had left his face now appears in two spots on his cheeks. 'I *told* you I didn't want to do this. I *told* you it was the wrong thing to do. I said we could get in a lot of trouble. Didn't I say that?'

'Yes,' I say in a small voice.

He drops his head into his hands and massages his temples. 'Unbelievable. This is so unbelievable.'

'I know. I'm so sorry.' I shift my chair around the side of the table to be closer to him. 'This guy is a terrible person. I hate that he's doing this to us.'

Luke grunts in response.

I drop my voice. 'If we got rid of him …'

I watch Luke's expression. Will he go for it? In the experiment by Milgram, more than half of the subjects administered the 450 V electric shock—a dose of electricity that would have proven fatal if it had been real. They didn't want to do it, but they did it. All because they were told to do it.

He lifts his face from his hands. 'I don't know what you're suggesting.'

'I think you do.' I pause meaningfully. 'It's our only choice, Luke.'

'It's not. It's really not.'

'As long as he's alive, he's going to hold this over us,' I say. 'You don't want that, do you? There's only one way to make sure he can't destroy us.'

'No. No way.'

'Think about it. What else can we do?' Luke looks ill. 'Please stop.'

'It's our only choice.'

He slams his palms against the table so hard that all the dishes shake. 'I'm not fucking killing anyone, Adrienne. Okay?'

I flinch in my seat. I've been dating Luke for four months, and I've never heard him raise his voice like that before. I don't think I've ever seen him this upset, but I can't say he doesn't have a right to be.

He pushes back his chair, the legs scraping against the floor. His face is bright red, and there's a blood vessel bulging in his temple. He won't even look at me. 'I need to get out of here.'

'Luke ...'

I try to reach for him, but he shakes me off roughly. He makes a beeline for my front door, and the whole house trembles as he slams it closed. I run to the door just in time to hear the engine of his car revving up. I crack the door open and watch his tail beams disappear into the distance.

That's it. He could forgive me for asking him to break into EJ's computer, but he won't forgive me for this. I saw it in his eyes—I pushed him too far. I'm not sure I'll ever see him again. I can't even blame him.

I've lost him. The first guy I ever loved, and I've screwed it all up.

I shut my front door and lean back against it. I let the tears run down my face, cursing the moment I laid eyes on EJ. I should have told his mother no. I knew he was trouble. I knew it from the second I saw him.

I've ruined my relationship with Luke, but I will not let him be a casualty of this monster. I'm going to take care of this problem. And I'm going to take care of it myself.

CHAPTER 42

TRICIA

PRESENT DAY

A more skilled liar may have been able to deny it. But this man is not a skilled liar. I can tell by the way the creases on his face deepen and what little colour he had in his cheeks completely vanishes. I hit the nail on the head.

This man is the same person I heard on the tape. The one who wanted to kiss Adrienne Hale.

'You're the boyfriend?' Ethan shakes the knife in his fist. 'You're the one who killed that shrink?'

The man, Luke, shakes his head vigorously. 'No, I … I mean, yes, fine, Adrienne was my girlfriend. But I didn't kill her. I *loved* her. I would never …'

Ethan narrows his eyes. 'So tell me what you're doing here.'

He rubs his hands on his blue jeans. 'It's what I said. I don't have a place to go, and this house was empty, so I've been staying here.'

'Why don't you have a place to go?'

'Because my life completely went to shit after the newspapers called me a murderer.' He lifts his eyes—I hadn't realized how bloodshot they look. 'They dragged my name through the mud. Over *nothing*. I didn't kill her. But my company let me go, and I couldn't find anything else. And my family wouldn't help me either. Even they thought that I ...' His voice breaks. 'So I'm unemployed and broke. That's my story.'

Ethan stares at the other man, his lips twisted into a frown. 'I don't believe you.'

Luke drops his arms. 'You don't believe me? What do you think I—'

'*Hands up in the air*.'

Luke freezes in the middle of a sentence. There's something in Ethan's voice, and he quickly puts his hands back in the air. 'Fine. Sorry. But I'm telling you the truth.'

'Or maybe ...' A vein pulses in Ethan's temple. 'Maybe you came here last night with a purpose. Maybe when you found out the house went up for sale, you knew you had to get rid of Adrienne Hale's body before some-body found it.'

Luke's jaw drops open. 'What? No. I had no idea that—'

'And when we left the house,' Ethan goes on, 'you were hoping you could quickly get rid of the body before we came back in.'

Luke looks almost sick. 'No. That's not ... Look, I didn't even know the body was here.'

'Yeah, right.'

'I didn't!' Luke starts to lower his hands, but at the expression on Ethan's face, he raises them higher. 'I had no idea. But when I heard the shouting, I thought … I had to see. Adrienne … She just disappeared. We were supposed to see each other that night. I don't … She wouldn't have just left. She wasn't like that.' He looks down at the floor, his features twisting with anguish. 'I loved her. And I never found out what happened to her.'

Tears spring to my eyes. He's telling the truth—that or his acting skills have improved significantly in the last ten minutes. But my husband's face remains impassive. 'Bullshit. I don't believe a word of this.'

'Ethan,' I say, 'I believe him.'

'Really?' His voice is dripping with condescension. This is the side of my husband that I've only seen a few times, and I don't particularly like it. 'So say we fall for his lies. Then what? We just let him wander the house and trust that he's such a nice guy he's not going to murder us while we sleep?'

He has a point. I believe Luke is harmless. But am I willing to bet my life on it?

No. I'm not.

'So what should we do?' I ask.

Ethan's eyes rake over the man standing in front of us. 'We tie him up.'

Luke stumbles backward at this revelation as panic fills his eyes. I wonder if he's thinking about trying to get away. I don't think he could. Ethan has the knife, and even if there wasn't a knife, Ethan could take Luke in a fight. My husband works out. He's got the big guns, which you can see peeking out under the bottom of the sleeves of that Yankees T-shirt. 'There's duct tape in the desk,' I recall. 'Do you want me to get it?' I don't want Ethan rifling through the desk and finding the cassette tapes.

'Yes.' Ethan shakes the knife at Luke. 'Lie down on the couch. *Now*.'

A chill goes down my spine at the way my husband is taking charge of this situation. I never imagined how Ethan would react in a high-intensity situation like this. I'm impressed.

Luke can tell Ethan isn't messing around. He obligingly stumbles over to the sofa and lies down on his back. I grab the duct tape out of the drawer and start by binding his legs. I wrap the duct tape around his ankles, just above his old Nike sneakers, which look like they used to be white and are now a muddy shade of gray.

'Now hold out your arms,' Ethan snaps at him.

Luke's eyes fill with dread. 'Please don't do this.'

'*Hold out your arms*.' Ethan nods in my direction.

'Tricia, make sure it's tight enough that he can't get out.'

I crouch beside Luke as I bind his hands together with the duct tape. I hazard a look at his face, and for a split second, our eyes meet. The shake of his head is barely perceptible. *Please don't do this*.

I look away. I don't have a choice. Ethan is right—we can't have him wandering around the house while we're trapped here.

I can breathe easier once Luke is bound on the couch. There won't be any more mysterious crashes around the house. I won't have to worry about somebody coming down from the attic to murder us.

'What are you going to do now?' Luke asks. Even though he's lying down, he looks incredibly uncomfortable—as you would imagine somebody with their wrists and ankles duct-taped together would be. He squirms, trying to adjust his position, but it's difficult for him.

'That's none of your goddamn business,' Ethan retorts. 'Come on, Tricia. Let's go.'

I follow Ethan out of the office, and he shuts the door behind us. It's only when the door is closed that he drops the arm holding the knife, which he places on a nearby bookshelf. All the tension seems to drain out of his body at once.

'We've got to get out of here,' he says. 'Like, tonight. I don't want to wait until the morning. I don't want to sleep under the same roof as that guy.'

'Me neither.' The thought of a man bound against his will in the room below us is very unsettling. I'll never be able to sleep. 'But what can we do?'

'I can go for help.'

My stomach sinks. 'Ethan, no …'

'Hear me out.' He holds up a finger. 'It's only about a mile to get to the main road. I can walk that far, then flag a car down for help. Or actually, I may have some phone reception over there. I might not even have to walk all the way to the main road if I can get my phone to work.' I look doubtfully out of one of the picture windows.

There is a *lot* of snow out there. Moreover, it's gotten very dark over the last hour. Pitch-black. There are no street- lights or lights from nearby houses or any lighting whatso-ever anywhere outside the premises. What if he gets lost?

What if he freezes to death?

I grab Ethan's arm, digging my fingernails into his skin. 'Please don't go.'

'I'll be fine,' he assures me with the confidence that I don't feel. 'I have a warm coat and a good pair of boots. I bet it will only take me about half an hour to get to the main road.'

'And you'd just leave me here?' A lump rises in my throat. 'With *him*?'

'He's contained. For now.'

I shake my head, but I can already see in Ethan's eyes how determined he is. There's no way I can talk him out of this.

'I'll be back in an hour—two, tops,' he says. 'I promise.'

I place my palm on my abdomen. It's still flat—no sign of a baby bump yet. In the coming months, it will grow larger and larger with the life we made blossoming inside me. As excited as I am about this journey, I don't want to do it alone. I can't imagine my life without Ethan.

'Please be careful,' I murmur.

'Don't worry,' he says. 'I'll be back in an hour.'

He leans in to kiss me, and as I feel his hot breath, I say a silent prayer. Please don't let this be the last time I see him. I will always blame myself if something happens to him.

'Don't go into the room for any reason.' Ethan's voice is stern. 'No matter what. Okay, Tricia?'

'Okay,' I agree.

'He's tied up. The only way he can hurt you is if you take the tape off his wrists and ankles.'

'I know.'

A flash of doubt passes over Ethan's face, but then he shakes his head. 'Okay, I'll see you soon.'

He starts to walk past me, but then he freezes in his steps. Something has caught his attention. Something by the stairwell.

I swivel my head, following his gaze. That's when I see what he's looking at. It's the bookcase by the stairs. The one that concealed the hidden room.

And it is now hanging ajar.

CHAPTER 43

I want to do something to try to distract Ethan from the hidden room, but his eyes are focused on it like a laser beam.

'What is *that*?' he says.

'I ... I don't know. Probably just a closet.'

But he's not listening to me. He strides over to the bookcase while my heart does jumping jacks in my chest. How could I be so stupid as to leave it open? I was sure I shut it the last time I went in to grab some tapes, but I noticed the latch doesn't always catch. It must've swung open again after I closed it.

And in a flash, Ethan is pulling open the door. I at least turned the light out, which delays him about five seconds as he fumbles around for the cord. When he finally finds it and the room lights up, I hear the sharp inhalation of his breath. 'What the ...?'

I stand at the entrance to the room, wringing my hands together. I want to pretend I don't know anything about this, but he'll see right through me.

Ethan selects one tape from a shelf. He examines the writing on the spine. 'She recorded all her patient interviews.'

'Yeah,' I say.

'There must be thousands of these.' His eyes rake over the shelves and shelves packed with tapes. 'When did you find this place?'

My cheeks feel like they're on fire. 'Um …'

'Tricia …'

'Yesterday. I found it yesterday.'

'And you didn't tell me?'

Obviously not. 'You seemed busy with work. I didn't think you would care.'

'That's a load of bullshit and you know it, Tricia.' Bright red creeps into his face from his neck. 'Have you been listening to these tapes?'

'No,' I answer quickly.

He raises his eyebrows. 'How about if you tell me the truth this time?'

'Maybe a couple …'

'*Don't lie.*' His voice is sharp now, not quite yelling but just on the verge. There's a glint in his eyes that makes me take a step back. 'Have you been listening to these tapes?'

'Not that many. Maybe five or six.'

I'm still lying. I listened to far more tapes than that. If Ethan went back into Dr Hale's office and looked in her desk drawer, he would see more tapes than that. I'm taking a chance he won't do that.

'Don't listen to any more tapes,' he says in a voice that doesn't sound like the man I married. 'Promise me you won't.'

'I promise,' I gasp.

He stands there for a moment, studying my face. I try not to squirm under his gaze. It's yet another reminder that I've only known this man for a little over a year. There's so much I still don't know about him, even though I've pledged to spend my life with him and I've got his child growing inside me. He doesn't want to share his past with me, and whenever I bring it up, he shuts down.

I'm his wife. He should feel comfortable telling me anything. It's upsetting that he feels there are things he can't tell me. That needs to change. Maybe not this minute, but everything needs to get laid out on the table. *Soon*. If we're starting a family together, there can't be any secrets.

Ethan finally rips his eyes away from my face. He turns around and closes the door to the hidden room. I hear the snap as it closes. When he turns back to look at me, the colour in his face has gone back to normal.

'I'm going out now to try to find help,' he says. 'I'll be back soon, okay?'

I nod, not wanting him to leave, although realizing it has to be this way.

He reaches out and grabs my arm hard enough that it hurts. But not enough to leave behind bruises. 'Don't go in that room again.'

'I won't . . .'

'I mean it.' His grip tightens. 'That's private patient information. We could get in a lot of trouble for listening to it. We should turn it over to the police.'

'Yes, of course.' But there's something in his eyes that tells me this isn't the reason he doesn't want me to listen to those tapes. He isn't being entirely honest with me.

He runs his tongue over his lips. 'How did you get it open anyway?'

'*The Shining*. I was going to read it, but it unlocked the door when I tried to pull it open.'

He considers this for a moment, then he nods. He yanks his black beanie out of his coat pocket and shoves it onto his golden hair. He's got on his black boots, and he stomps across the living room on his way to the front door. He gives me one last look before he slams the door shut behind him.

The sound of the door slamming echoes through the giant living room. For a full minute after he's gone, I just stand there, trying to figure out my next move.

Ethan knows about the hidden room with the cassette tapes in it. I don't know if he's going to make good on his promise to tell the police about it, but if there's any chance of that, I've got to put back all the tapes I removed from the room. I don't want to be accused of tampering with evidence.

There's only one problem.

If I want those tapes, I have to go back into Dr Hale's office.

CHAPTER 44

This is not a big deal. All I have to do is walk into the office, take the tapes out of the desk and put them in my coat pocket, then leave the room.

I don't have to talk to Luke. I don't have to interact with him. He's tied up—there's no way he can hurt me.

I hate the idea of doing this while Ethan is gone. And it's not like he's upstairs or something. He's not even in the house. He's not reachable by phone. If Luke tries to attack me, it will just be me and him in the house.

But he won't attack me. I used plenty of duct tape. He's probably exactly like he was when I left him. Lying on the couch, helpless. I'd bet my life on it.

And I can't possibly wait for Ethan to come back. What if he comes back with the police? I have a feeling he won't, but if he does, I'm screwed.

I approach the door to the office. I press my ear against it, listening for any ominous sounds. I don't hear anything. But that doesn't necessarily mean anything.

Ethan left that knife on one of the bookshelves. I debate bringing it with me into the room but then decide against it. Luke is tied up. I should be fine.

I place my hand on the doorknob, too chicken to turn it. I count to three, take a deep breath, and twist the knob. Then I push the door open.

The room is mostly how we left it. The compartment in the floor is still closed. The couch is still askew on the other side of the room. And Luke is still on the sofa, his wrists and ankles bound with duct tape. The only difference is he's managed to work himself into a sitting position. It makes me uneasy. If he could go from lying to sitting, then he could go from sitting to standing. And then what? Ethan was right to go for help. I don't feel comfortable spending the night with this man under the same roof.

Luke jerks his head up when I enter the room. He stares at me with those bloodshot eyes with deep purple circles underneath.

'I just need to get something,' I mumble. I'm not sure why I felt the need to offer him an explanation.

'I won't get in the way,' he says.

I grunt in response.

The setup of the room is awkward. The way the couch has been moved, I have to squeeze past Luke to get to the desk. His eyes are on me, watching me as I draw closer to him.

'Your name is Tricia, right?' he says.

I don't make eye contact or respond to his question. 'Listen, Tricia.' He clears his crackly throat. 'My fingers are starting to tingle. I don't know if there's any way you could do me a favour and make the tape a little looser?'

I snort. 'You must think I'm the dumbest person on the planet.'

Despite everything, Luke lets out a little chuckle. 'Worth a try.'

I glance over in his direction, and one side of his lips is pulled up in a lopsided smile. He's not as handsome as my husband, but I could see how he'd be cute if he got a shave and a haircut—and took a long shower. For a second, I catch a glimpse of the Luke who was on that tape I listened to. The one who Dr Adrienne Hale fell in love with.

If only she hadn't. Maybe everything would have been different.

I squeeze past him to get to the desk. I pull open the drawer where I stashed the tapes, and sure enough, they're still there. I want to stuff them into my coat pocket, but Luke is staring at me, barely blinking. He won't look away.

'Is there something you have to say?' I snap at him.

'Actually, yes.'

I fold my arms across my chest. 'I'm not taking off the duct tape. Don't bother asking. You're going to sit right there until the police get here and you can explain how Adrienne Hale's body got under the floor of her office.'

'Yeah, that's the thing.' Luke leans back against the couch. 'I don't think … I mean, I'm pretty sure that isn't Adrienne under the floorboards.'

I freeze. 'What?'

'You heard me.'

He doesn't know what he's talking about. He's just trying to scare me. He knows it's just the two of us in the house, and he's trying to manipulate me. That's what this is. I shouldn't even engage him.

'I thought it was her at first,' he says. 'I mean, who else could it be? I didn't even want to look because … I just couldn't bear it. I don't care what the paper said about me—I *loved* Adrienne. I would have married her, except …'

'So why do you think it isn't her?'

I don't know how anyone could tell. That body in there—you can't even tell if it was a male or female, much less their specific identity.

'They still had clothing on.' He grimaces. 'Scraps of it anyway … I assume most of the material disintegrated. And you could tell they were wearing a pair of blue jeans. But Adrienne never wore blue jeans. She hated them. She wouldn't have been caught … well, you know. So I don't see how that could be her.'

I swallow. 'Maybe she was having a laundry day and decided to wear blue jeans.'

'She didn't even *own* any.' He shakes his head. 'The shirt didn't look familiar to me either. That's not her under the floor. I'd bet anything.'

Both of us turn to look at the rectangular outline on the floor. He's right about the blue jeans. I looked through a bunch of her drawers, and she didn't seem to own any.

'Do you know who it is then?' Luke hesitates. 'Yes. I think I do.'

A chill runs down my spine. I don't care if Luke sees what I'm doing or not at this point—I just need to get out of this room. I open the drawer and start stuffing the tapes in my pockets. He's watching me do it, but he doesn't comment.

'I didn't kill her, Tricia,' he says quietly. 'I would never do something like that.'

I slam the drawer shut. 'That's for the police to decide, not me.'

I squeeze past him, my pockets bulging with all the tapes I stole from the hidden room. I've still got plenty of time before Ethan returns, but I don't want to take any chances. By the time he gets back, I want the room to be exactly the way I found it.

I'm used to the drill by now. I tilt forward the copy of *The Shining*, and I hear the click as the door unlocks. I pull it open and tug on the cord to turn on the light.

One by one, I replace the tapes on the shelves. I've got a whole handful of EJ tapes, and I've got to organize them back in the order I found them. I've got a few other random ones, and I make sure those are put back as well. When I'm done, I've got only one tape left in my pocket. I reach my hand into my pocket and feel the rectangular object inside. I squeeze on it so hard that the case cracks under my grip.

I will leave this room exactly the way I found it. Every tape is in the same place it was when I first walked in here.

Every tape except one.

CHAPTER 45

TRANSCRIPT OF RECORDING

This is session #185 with PL, a twenty-seven-year-old female experiencing PTSD after surviving an extremely traumatic incident.

PL: 'Dr Hale, I just wanted to let you know I'm going to be moving soon.'

DH: 'Oh? Where are you moving to?'

PL: 'I got a job in Manhattan.'

DH: 'Oh wow. I didn't even realize you were interviewing.'

PL: 'Well, my mother always says, if opportunity doesn't knock, build a door.'

DH: 'Your mother sure has some great sayings.'

PL: 'Yes, she sure does! Anyway, I'm looking at some apartments there—hoping to find a decent one-bedroom.'

DH: 'That's wonderful. Congratulations.'

PL: 'Thank you so much. I just wanted to tell you because it will mean we won't be able to have our sessions any more.'

DH: 'Of course. I understand. This is a big move for you.'

PL: 'It is. And I couldn't have done it without you. You've been amazing, Dr Hale.'

DH: 'I'm glad I've helped you.'

PL: 'You really have. I could barely leave my house when I first met you, and now I'm moving to Manhattan. I feel like I can finally put the whole thing behind me.'

DH: 'Yes. That's very healthy.'

PL: 'And maybe one day, they'll catch the bastard who murdered my fiancé and my friends.'

DH: 'Hmm. I don't think so.'

PL: 'You may be right. I mean, after all this time, it would be too much to hope—'

DH: 'No. That's not why they won't catch him.'

PL: 'Oh. Well, then why not?'

DH: 'The reason they won't catch him is that he doesn't exist.'

PL: 'What?'

DH: 'It's hard to arrest a man who is entirely fictional, isn't it?'

PL: '*Excuse* me?'

DH: 'You heard me.'

PL: 'I … What are you saying, Dr Hale?'

DH: 'I think you know what I'm saying.'

PL: 'I'm afraid I don't.'

DH: 'I'm saying you made the whole thing up. There never was a man at the cabin. You murdered your fiancé and your friends, and you made up a fictional assailant.'

PL: 'I was *stabbed*!'

DH: 'Barely. You did it to yourself so it would look realistic. Nobody would believe that a man came into the cabin and stabbed everyone but you, so you had no choice.'

PL: 'This is … it's insane. How could you think I made it all up?'

DH: 'Because you did. Do you think I can't spot a liar a mile away?'

PL: 'But why would I do something like that?'

DH: 'I haven't entirely worked it out. I suspect Cody was cheating on you with Alexis, and you decided to teach them both a lesson. And Megan was an unfortunate casualty of the whole thing. That's my suspicion based on the fact that she died much quicker than the other two.'

PL: 'I …'

DH: 'Guessed right, did I?'

PL: 'This is … I mean, I've been coming here for *three years*. You included me in your book.'

DH: 'Well, it was a good story. Incredibly compelling. I'd say you can't make this stuff up, but obviously you can.'

PL: 'This is insane.'

DH: 'Don't look at me like that. I'm not the only one who suspected you. Detective Gardner thought you did it also, but he couldn't prove it. Except he didn't have a window into your thoughts the way I have. He hasn't been collecting little inconsistencies over the last three years.'

PL: 'This is ridiculous. I'm leaving.'

DH: 'Yes, you should leave. I'd like some privacy to give the detective a call.'

PL: 'Wait. Hang on.'
DH: 'I thought you were leaving?'
PL: 'Okay. *Okay*.'
DH: 'So you admit it?'
PL: 'What do you want, Dr Hale?'
DH: 'I have a little problem. And I need your help.'
PL: 'What kind of problem?'
DH: 'There's somebody who's been causing me some trouble. I'd like to take care of it, but I can't do it myself.'
PL: 'Well, what do you want *me* to do?'
DH: 'Oh, I think you know, Patricia.'

CHAPTER 46

(PA)TRICIA

PRESENT DAY

I'm not a murderer.

Okay, technically I am. But when I imagine somebody being a murderer, I imagine something different. I imagine somebody evil, who goes around killing good people for no reason.

I killed my fiancé, Cody. But he wasn't a good person. We were supposed to get married in two months. Two months! The wedding invitations had gone out already. I had plastered photos of me holding up my gorgeous diamond ring all over Instagram. We had already registered at half a dozen places, and some of the gifts had even come in already.

Then I found out Cody was sleeping with my best friend, Alexis.

Do you know what it feels like when someone betrays you like that? The love of my life and my best friend. Going at it like rabbits. Right under my nose, because they thought I was too stupid to find out about it. And I might not have—if that text message from Alexis didn't pop up on Cody's phone while he was in the bathroom. Yes, they were that careless.

I knew the code to his phone, and I typed it in the next night while he was sleeping. I found out Alexis and Cody had been messing around together since shortly after the engagement. That it was *serious*. He was planning to break off the engagement to be with her, but he was worried about how I might take it.

She's not the most stable person in the world, he wrote to her. That was unfair. I was stable. Anyone would have cracked if they found out that their fiancé was thinking about ending their engagement to be with their best friend only two months before the wedding. I can't imagine anything more humiliating than that. I would have had to call all my guests and explain that the wedding was off, and of course, many of them would ask what happened, and I'd have to lie and say we just weren't right for each other. But of course, everyone online would be whispering about it. So nobody could blame me for doing what I did.

Honestly, anyone in a similar situation probably *wishes* they had done what I did.

Alexis was probably snickering to herself when I told her about the cabin Cody and I rented, which had an extra two bedrooms. *Why don't you and Megan come along?* I suggested.

I had to invite Megan, even though she hadn't technically done anything wrong. It would've been suspicious if I only invited Alexis. And to be fair, I never liked Megan much. She was one of those people who always put everyone down every chance she got. The world is better off without her. Trust me.

I brought a bottle of tequila, some limes, and a salt shaker. I also brought a dime bag of weed. I made sure everyone in the room got good and wasted. I wouldn't have a chance to take them all down otherwise. After all, it was one against three.

I picked a night when I knew it would rain. I was worried that if they didn't see a fifth set of footprints, nobody would believe my story. But if it was raining, the soil all around the cabin turned to mud.

I had to do it one by one. I took care of Megan first, on the porch, because I didn't want to draw that one out. I told her I needed to talk to her about something outside, and then the second we were in the woods, I took the knife out of my jacket and slashed her throat.

Cody was next. I did it right in the bed where we were sleeping. There was a moment after I stabbed him three times, just before he lost consciousness, when I whispered in his ear, '*That's what you get for messing around behind my back.*' I wanted him to know why I did it—wanted that to be his last thought before he died.

Then came Alexis. I was the angriest with her. She had been my best friend since we were *five years old*. How could she do it to me? I let her die slowly, bleeding all over the floor while she begged for help.

I was last. Nobody would believe my story if I were completely uninjured, so I read about where to place the knife to avoid serious injury. When I showed up at the police station, soaking wet and sobbing about the intruder in the cabin, most of the blood I was caked in wasn't mine. I played the part so well. Honestly, I deserve an Academy Award for that performance. My parents and sister never doubted for a moment that we had been a victim of a vicious attack by a psychopath in the woods. Only that awful detective suspected I might be lying, but he couldn't prove it. As far as everyone was concerned, I was the victim.

No, I was a *hero*. Because I survived.

My mother was the one who insisted on the sessions with Dr Hale. *Dr Hale is the best*. And she always said nothing is more important than mental health.

So I agreed to go. And it was fun. Even though I wasn't the victim of a psychopath in the woods, I was still traumatized by the entire experience. I mean, having to kill your boyfriend and your best friend does a number on your head, although it's not like they left me with much of a choice. Dr Hale knew just what to say though. And I sort of enjoyed the game by that point. The deception.

I had no clue she saw through my entire charade.

So you can imagine how I felt when she told me she was onto me. She mentioned recording our sessions at the beginning of therapy, and I think I even signed some sort of consent form. It didn't seem like a big deal to me. But once she revealed what she knew, I thought back to all my sessions, mentally reviewing all my slip-ups.

I had to do what she asked of me. I had no choice.

CHAPTER 47

ADRIENNE

BEFORE

It's well past midnight when the Audi pulls up in front of my house.

It's the same car my former agent Paige drove, but the car belongs to Patricia. I'm sure her parents bought it for her—they have spoiled her horribly since she returned from that cabin, dripping wet and covered in blood. I watch from my window as Patricia climbs out of her car, dressed in a skimpy, skintight red dress that just barely covers her underwear. She slams the door closed with more force than she needed to use. I permanently dismantled the camera looking down on the front door so there would be no record of who's entering and leaving the house tonight. I realized Patricia was lying to me during her very first appointment. Not to say that she wasn't a skilled liar, because she is. She puts on quite the show. But I'm even more skilled at picking out the cues that somebody is untruthful. Like EJ, Patricia has a tell. When she's going to lie, she crosses her right leg over her left.

I suspect the detective involved in the case knew she was lying as well. But it's one thing to know it in your gut, and it's another thing to prove it. Detective Gardner couldn't prove that Patricia killed her fiancé and two of her closest friends. So she got away with it. Not only that but she was praised as being the victim who got away.

But Patricia Lawton isn't a victim. When she found out her best friend was cheating on her with her fiancé, she didn't let either of them get away with it. Over the last three years, I have informally diagnosed her with antisocial personality disorder, based on her impaired empathy for other people, her aggressive and criminal behaviour, as well as her history of lying and deception. Like many other people with antisocial personality disorder, Patricia is charming and attractive, with above-average intelligence. If she didn't have that going for her, she might not have gotten away with it.

There have been several clues over the years to her diagnosis. When her grandmother died from a heart attack last year, she cried very convincing tears during our session, but she didn't mention that she had been the one responsible for helping Grammy with her heart medications—I only found out when I called Mrs Lawton to express my condolences. She also failed to mention the considerable estate she inherited. When I asked Patricia about it during her next session, she crossed her right leg over her left and told me how terrible she felt that she might have gotten her grandmother's medications mixed up.

Mrs Lawton was always a trove of information about her daughter's troubled history. Playmates with mysterious injuries. Pets that died suddenly. *Poor Tricia has had such bad luck*.

On some level, I'm sure Mrs Lawton knows what her daughter is. She's not a stupid woman. But denial is a powerful defense mechanism. I could hear the relief in her voice when she told me the stories—finally unburdening herself and passing the buck on to me.

And I knew exactly what to do with this information.

When I open the front door to greet Patricia, she doesn't look happy. She's tugging on the too-short hem of her skirt and glares at me under my porch lights. 'He's in the car.'

'Still passed out?'

'Yes. But he's waking up.'

'Did you have any trouble?'

'No. It was easy.'

Despite her being so pissed off at me, I believe on some level Patricia enjoyed the challenge I gave her. She dolled herself up, drove to the casino, and sidled up next to EJ at the poker table. Just like in his fantasy, she didn't even tell him her name. Then she lured him to her vehicle with the promise of going back to her place. I told her exactly what to say.

During the car ride, he would have become more and more drowsy from what Patricia had slipped into his drink at the casino, until he finally lost consciousness. I swear, it gets easier every time I drug EJ. You would think he would see it coming by now.

'Did you check him out of the hotel?' I ask.

'Yes. I used his phone.' She looks down at her fingernails, which are painted blood red. 'And I moved his Porsche to another lot with long-term parking. He's paid up for a month.'

EJ has no friends and no job. His parents are gone. Nobody will even notice him missing for weeks if not months.

I follow Patricia to her Audi. A dark shadow of a man occupies the back seat. That's him. She did it. She really did it. She did what Luke couldn't—or wouldn't—do.

'I duct-taped his hands together,' she tells me. 'I did his legs too, but there's a bit more give so he can walk. I stuck a piece over his mouth, but you can't see it because he's got the sack on his head.'

She's got guts—I'll give her that. She drove all the way here from Connecticut with a man tied up in the back seat. Yes, it was the middle of the night. But if she had gotten pulled over, that would've been the end.

'I only tied him up about twenty minutes ago,' she says, as if reading my thoughts. 'He started stirring, and I didn't want to take a chance.'

'His phone?'

Patricia reaches into her purse and pulls it out. She drops it into my waiting hand.

I squint down at the black screen in the darkness. 'You powered it down?'

'I did. But I've heard they can sometimes track a phone as long as it still has a battery. So be careful.'

I'll be very careful. I fully intend to pulverize this phone until it's unrecognizable.

When we get closer, I see the paper sack on EJ's head. The paper crinkles slightly as he shifts in his seat. It's hard to tell how awake he is since he's immobilized. I sort of hope he's awake for this next part.

Patricia pulls the back door open. Now I can see the duct tape securing EJ's hands together. She kicks him in the calf with her high heels, hard enough to leave behind a bruise.

'Get up!' she barks at him.

His head snaps up, but he can't get out of the car without help. She kicks him again, and he groans, but he still doesn't move.

I end up grabbing his legs and shifting them outside the vehicle. He still can't get up on his own without the two of us hauling him to his feet. Muffled noises come from inside the paper bag. His light-gray T-shirt has sweat stains under his armpits.

We walk him into my house and into my office. Because his ankles are partially bound together, he has terrible balance and has to walk with small, shuffling steps. When we get into the office, Patricia stops short. She looks around. 'Did you change something in here?'

'No,' I say.

She cocks her head to the side. She is certain something is different, but she can't put her finger on what it is. I know what it is though. I moved the sofa. But she doesn't need to know that part. It's better she doesn't know.

Once inside the office, I attempt to get EJ to sit on the sofa, but between the duct tape on his wrist and ankles and the bag on his head, he misses it completely. He goes crashing to the floor—hard. Patricia frowns.

'Do you want me to help you get him up?' she asks.

I shake my head. It's easier that he's on the floor. 'I'm fine. You can leave now.'

She narrows her eyes. 'What are you going to do?'

'It's none of your concern.'

She taps one of her heels on the wooden floor. If she were only two feet to the left, she would have heard the difference in sound that the floor made and discovered my secret. 'I believe it's partially my concern. I'm the one who got him here after all.'

'Don't worry,' I say. 'I'll take care of it.'

'I don't mind helping. As my mother always says, if we always helped one another, no one would need luck.'

I'll just bet she doesn't mind. 'It's fine. I've got it under control.'

A flicker of curiosity passes over her pretty features. 'What are you going to do with him?'

'I promise—nobody will find him.'

She pouts for a second but then throws up her hands. 'Fine. Do what you want, Dr Hale.'

She flicks her honey-blonde hair over her shoulder, then storms out of the office. On her way out, she looks up at the portrait she gave me, which is hanging over the mantel. She flashes me a disdainful look.

'I can't believe you hung that giant portrait of yourself right in your living room.' She sneers at me. 'You're just as arrogant as I thought you were.'

'I like it,' I say pleasantly. I can afford to be pleasant at the moment, when the source of all my problems is lying in a crumpled heap on the floor of my office.

I lead Patricia to my front door and lock it behind her when she leaves. Patricia has been in my house many times in the last three years, but this will be the last time. I'm not going to ask any other favours from this girl. She acts sweet but I know the truth—she's dangerous.

And now that she's gone, I can finish up here.

When I get back to the office, EJ is still lying on the floor. He's awake now, squirming to get out of his duct tape restraints, although Patricia tied him up very well.

I walk over to him, standing over his wriggling body. Finally, I reach down and yank the paper bag off his head. The adrenaline has overpowered whatever medications Patricia gave him. His eyes are open wide, and his T-shirt is now drenched with sweat, even though it's a bit chilly here. His lips are moving under the duct tape, but no intelligible sounds come out. I watch as a dark stain spreads across his crotch.

I crouch beside him. 'Hello there.'

He makes a muffled sound behind the duct tape on his lips.

I look into his gray eyes, unable to suppress a smile. 'I thought about your offer. And I decided you were right. I *would* like the two of us to spend a little time together.'

I grin. 'And I think it *will* be fun for me.'

His eyes are almost popping out of their sockets. I wonder if Luke would enjoy this as much as I am if he were here. If he were standing next to me right now, what would his reaction be?

I close my eyes for a moment, imagining it. I picture Luke's face staring down at EJ lying helpless on the floor.

Even in my imagination, Luke isn't smiling. He wouldn't approve of this. He doesn't have the stomach for it.

'That guy broke up with me because of you, you know,' I say to EJ. Luke hasn't officially broken it off with me, but it's been a week, he won't pick up the phone when I call, and he hasn't answered any of my text messages. You don't have to have an MD and a PhD to figure out that one. He wants nothing to do with me any more. Apparently, asking him to commit murder was a deal-breaker. But I suppose I shouldn't be surprised. People like me are destined to end up alone.

'He was a great guy,' I tell him, although I'm not even sure I'm talking to him any more. 'He was sweet and smart, and he overlooked all my faults. No, he didn't overlook them—he *liked* them. He loved me for all the things about me that weren't perfect.' I take a gulping breath, pushing back the tears gathering in my eyes. I won't give him the satisfaction. 'I really liked him. I *loved* him. And because of you, I lost him. Because you're a selfish asshole who decided to screw up my entire life.'

EJ is trying to say something. It might be 'I'm sorry.' But it might also be 'Go to hell.' It's hard to tell with the duct tape on his mouth.

Honestly, I don't care what he's saying. It doesn't matter.

I straighten up. I draw back my right foot, and EJ flinches, realizing I'm about to kick him in the gut. But then at the last second, I don't do it.

Instead, I walk over to the corner of the room where the leather sofa used to be. I moved it this morning. One thing that charmed me about this house when I first bought it was the hidden panel under the floor in this room. The real estate agent told me about it with a proud smile. *You could hide valuables down there*.

I've kept things down there over the years, but I cleared it all out this morning. I need all the room in there that I can get.

There's a tiny hook in the floorboard that's barely visible to the naked eye—it blends right into the rest of the floor. I hook my fingers into it and pull it open to reveal the space inside. Just large enough for a human body to fit. The real estate agent told me that too, but she was joking. She laughed about it.

Did I know when I bought this house that I would eventually use the space to conceal a human body? I don't know. On some level, I must have considered it.

EJ's eyes bulge. He knows what's about to happen, and there's nothing he can do to stop it. I smile down at him. 'Actually,' I say, 'I don't think we're going to be spending that much time together. You're going to be spending a lot of time alone, as it turns out.'

It takes three rolls for me to get EJ into the space under the floor. He's squirming and kicking the whole time, but Patricia tied him up too tightly. He can't get free. As soon as he falls into the space, I can see the panic in his eyes ramp up several notches. I don't know if he believed until this minute that I was actually going to do it.

He is screaming now, although the sound is dampened by the duct tape over his lips. I watch him for a moment, then I lower the panel again, concealing the hiding space under the floor. Once again, you can't even tell it's there. Except for the muffled sounds coming from the floorboards.

That won't do at all.

I had intended to leave him there and allow nature to take its course. But this is too big a risk. He's too noisy. So I take the rest of the roll of duct tape Patricia gave me and start taping the edges of the panel. Effectively cutting off the oxygen supply.

I sit down on the couch and listen. The muffled sounds grow softer. It doesn't sound like screams any more. Whimpers, maybe. Crying, possibly. The sounds become quieter and quieter. Until they stop completely.

'Goodbye, Edward,' I say.

CHAPTER 48

TRICIA

PRESENT DAY

I didn't know for sure that Dr Hale was going to kill Edward Jamison. When somebody forces you to drug a guy, bind his wrists and ankles, and stick a bag over his head, you know they're not planning anything *good*. But I thought … well, maybe she just wanted to throw a scare into the guy.

I got in the habit of checking online for mentions of his name. Jamison had a public Facebook page, and every day, I would look for updates, but I never saw any. It was over a month later that I found the news article about his disappearance. And that's when I knew.

She killed him.

I was not entirely surprised to find out that Dr Adrienne Hale was capable of murder. There was something about her. Something in those intense green eyes. Hell, it seemed like if she concentrated hard enough, she could kill you with her mind alone.

The ironic thing is I went to Dr Hale complaining about sleep problems, but that got a lot worse after what she made me do for her. Yes, I had already killed several people, but I did it on my own terms. I had no idea what she did to Edward Jamison, and that was what drove me insane. I didn't even know where the body was.

She had already screwed me over once. I didn't trust her. I lay awake at night, obsessing over Dr Adrienne Hale.

I finally couldn't take it any more.

CHAPTER 49

ADRIENNE

BEFORE

I don't have any trouble at all finding parking at the free clinic today.

It's a good thing because I have a jam-packed schedule today. This isn't even my usual day to be here, and I'm seeing patients till nearly seven o'clock at night. I've been gone for over a month, on a tour to promote *The Anatomy of Fear*, which recently hit number eight on the *New York Times* bestseller list. Nobody knows that the account of the woman who survived a stabbing in an isolated cabin is entirely a lie.

It's been nearly four months since EJ, also known as Edward Jamison, left my life. Or rather, I should say, since he became a permanent part of my life. I peeled the duct tape off the floor later that day, destroyed his phone, and moved the couch back in place, but over the next several days, the stench coming from the floor became unbearable. I had to close off the room and cancel all my patients. I didn't go into my office for two months.

If I even got close to the door to my former office, the smell was enough to turn my stomach. But then, when I returned home from my book tour, I was relieved to find that the smell had abated significantly, although it was still very much present.

I finally went online and purchased a spray that was advertised to 'chemically neutralize odors from dead bodies.' I opened all the windows, aggressively spritzed the neutralizing chemical, and to my surprise and immense relief, it worked—the odor disappeared. You would never know there was a dead body down there.

I had assumed that at some point, the police would come by, asking questions about his disappearance. I even had a story ready. There were moments during my tour when I was signing books and I was certain the police would approach me with handcuffs and haul me away. But it never happened. Nobody even asked me any questions about him. And now, four months later, I'm starting to believe they might never come. After all, there was no cash trail for EJ's visits to my practice. The only person besides him who knew that he came to see me was his mother, and she's gone.

I got away with it. I killed a man, he's lying under the floorboards in my home, and nobody knows it but me. Well, Patricia likely knows I killed him but she doesn't know where the body is.

Patricia. So far, she hasn't been a problem. But it worries me that she knows what I've done. That we share this secret. Could she use it against me someday? I do not know. The secret I know about her is just as bad, possibly worse. I can't obsess over it anyway. Right now,

I've got to catch up on the patients I wasn't able to see during my book tour, and I've still got plenty of signings and television appearances on the books over the next several weeks. When I get into the clinic, Gloria is sitting at the front desk, humming to herself like she often does. When she sees me, her entire face lights up. 'I've got a surprise for you, Dr Hale.'

'Oh?' It's probably food. Patients love to bring sweets for me. I rarely eat them. Mostly, it's homemade items or cheap chocolates. I don't care how many comments Gloria makes about me needing to put meat on my bones— I'm not eating homemade goods prepared by psychiatric patients.

'It's in the documentation office,' she says. And she winks at me. 'You should go there right now.'

I follow Gloria's cryptic instructions and head to the documentation room. I'm guessing it's doughnuts. Patients love to bring in doughnuts. I skipped breakfast this morning, so I suppose I wouldn't mind a munchkin or two. Just this one time, I'll live dangerously.

But when I get to the room, I discover what Gloria was excited about. It's not doughnuts.

It's Luke.

I stare at him for a moment, my heart pounding. I haven't seen him in nearly five months, since that day he stormed out of my house after I asked him to … Well, we all know what I asked him to do. I had forgotten quite how handsome he is. He's clean-shaven, his dark brown hair newly clipped, wearing a freshly ironed dress shirt and a brown tie. And he's wearing that aftershave again. The same brand he was wearing the first night we were together.

Luke looks up from his computer at the sound of my footsteps in the entranceway to the room. He sucks in a breath when he sees me. 'Adrienne …'

'Oh.' I tuck a stray strand of hair behind my ear. 'I … I didn't expect you to be here.'

'Just had to do a software update.' He coughs into his hand. 'You usually come on Tuesdays. So I figured Thursday you wouldn't be here.'

'I'm working an extra day.' I hate how formal we sound when we're talking to each other. Like we're strangers. Like we didn't almost move in together. Like he isn't the first man I have ever fallen in love with. 'I'm playing catch up after my book tour.'

'Right.' He bobs his head. 'I saw your book came out. Congratulations.'

'Thank you. You didn't … Did you read it?'

He hesitates for a beat. 'Yes. I did. It was really good. Better than your last book even.' 'You think so?'

'I wouldn't lie.'

'Well.' I plaster a smile on my lips. 'Thank you.' 'You're welcome.'

We both stare for a moment, the air between us heavy with everything that happened the last time we saw each other. When he stormed out of my house.

Finally, he blurts out, 'I miss you.'

A lump rises in my throat. 'You do?'

'I really do.' He stands up and leans against the desk. 'A lot. You have no idea …'

I attempt to swallow the lump. 'I took care of that … situation. I paid him off.'

A lie, of course. I wonder if Luke knows it. Maybe he's decided not to care.

'I shouldn't have run out on you like that.' He adjusts his glasses on his nose. 'I know you didn't really mean that we should … I mean, I should've helped you figure out the situation. I just got freaked out. I'm sorry.'

'I forgive you.' I clear my throat. 'And … I miss you too. A *lot*.'

His shoulders sag. 'I'm so glad to hear that. Honestly, I haven't been able to stop thinking about you the last few months. I tried—believe me, I tried. But it's no use. I can't even sleep at night because I keep tossing and turning, thinking about how I blew it with the best woman I ever met.'

I arch an eyebrow. 'I could call in a prescription for some Ambien.'

He reaches over and takes my hand in his larger hands. I missed this feeling. 'Or you could have dinner with me tonight.

My lips stretch into a smile. 'I'm going to have a late night at the clinic tonight.'

'I can wait.' He leans in toward me. 'Also, I have a confession to make. I wasn't entirely truthful with you.'

My stomach flips. Does he know what I did to EJ? 'You weren't?'

He grins. 'The truth is, I knew you were going to be working today. Gloria told me. I asked her what days you would be in this week before I planned my schedule.'

That's his confession—that he was trying to see me. My knees wobble with relief. I grab his shirt collar and pull him toward me, then I press my lips against his. The way he kisses me back, I know he's been missing me as much as I've missed him.

He'll never know what I've done. I'm going to keep it that way.

Luke and I are meeting tonight at nine o'clock. I tried to finish up the clinic as quickly as I could, leaving behind a stack of paperwork at the end. I'll probably have to come back tomorrow, but Gloria was nice about it. She knew I made plans with Luke, and she was practically shooing me out the door.

Luke is picking me up at my house, then we're going out to a restaurant. As much as I'd like to have him inside the house, there's no way I'm allowing him inside while that body is still underneath my floorboards. Even though the smell seems to have abated, I swear I can still detect a faint whiff of death, especially in my office. I can't risk having him in the house. If he knows what I've done, he'll never forgive me.

Eventually, I've got to get rid of the body. I'm dreading it. It's like when I was a child and I used to smash large insects with a heavy book. I knew eventually I would have to pick up the book and clean up the smashed insect. But I always dreaded it.

I may not be perfect, but I'm not a psychopath. I didn't want to kill EJ. He gave me no choice.

I drive down the dark path to my house, keeping my eye on the clock. I've got an hour to shower and change before Luke arrives. I'll come up with an excuse for why he can't go inside the house. Perhaps I had it newly painted. I'm sure he'll believe whatever excuse I come up with. I may be good at detecting lies, but he is not.

And eventually, I'll have to get rid of the body for good. Maybe in a few more months. Nobody will be looking for him by then.

As I draw closer to my house, I see an Audi parked in front. My agent Paige's car. I wonder if she's come to beg me to take her back. If she has, she's wasting her time. It's far too late for that.

But then I see a dark figure leaning against the car—one I haven't seen in four months and hoped to never see again. A figure with long, shapely legs and silky blonde hair that gleams in the moonlight. It's Patricia Lawton. I forgot she drove the same kind of car as my former agent did.

I park my car next to the Audi and kill the engine. I stuff my keys in my purse and get out of the car. I don't know what Patricia wants, but I don't have time for it. I need time to look my best for Luke.

'Hi, Dr Hale,' she says. 'It's been a while, hasn't it?'

'Yes.'

Her teeth almost glow in the moonlight as she smiles. 'I was hoping we could talk.'

I glance down at my watch pointedly. 'I'm in a bit of a rush.'

'It'll just take a moment.'

I nod. 'We can talk out here. You've got one minute.'

'I just ...' She chews at her thumbnail, which is gnawed down to the quick. 'I'm nervous about what we did. What if somebody traces it back to us?'

'That won't happen. It's been months. Nobody is looking for him.'

'They might. If they find the body.'

'They won't.'

'You don't know for sure. And I've been thinking about it ...' Her lips twist downward. 'There's video footage in the casino. If they find out when he disappeared, they could look at the footage and figure out I was the one talking to him right before. They might see us leaving together. Or maybe they'll have footage from the garage.' She might be right. It's another reason Patricia has become a liability. I'll have to do something about it. But not now. 'I wouldn't worry about it.'

'I just want to know ...' Her eyes lock with mine. 'What did you do with his body?'

'What?' I almost choke. 'Patricia, I am not going to have this discussion with you. Trust me. Everything is fine.'

'I want to know where the body is. I need to know. Please tell me.'

I grunt in disgust. 'Your minute is up. I have to go.'

'Is it in the house somewhere?'

I hesitate a beat too long, and her eyes widen.

'You have the body in the house?' she gasps. 'My God. Where is it?'

'I can't discuss this with you.'

'But, Dr Hale—'

'Look.' I pause one more minute to address her. That's all she gets—I can't babysit this girl any longer. 'The only people who know about this are the two of us. All we have to do is keep the secret.'

Patricia's eyes don't blink once as she stares into mine. 'My mother always says the only way two people can keep a secret,' she says, 'is if one of them is dead.'

And then her fingers bite into my arm. A cold feeling comes over me, and I realize I have made a terrible mistake. I should never have gotten Patricia involved in this. I knew exactly how dangerous she was.

And now I am going to pay the price. Please forgive me, Luke …

CHAPTER 50

TRICIA

PRESENT DAY

Adrienne Hale is hardly the first person I have killed. Not even close.

The first was a girl named Whitney Young. She tormented me when I was sixteen years old, like only teenage girls do. She spread rumours about me all over the school and stole my best friend. She even convinced a cute boy named Victor (who I later discovered was Whitney's boyfriend) to ask me out on a date, then brought everyone to the coffee shop where we were supposed to meet so they could laugh at my humiliation when he stood me up. The funny part is that it was *Victor* who took the fall when Whitney's body washed up in a nearby river. We could all agree they both deserved it though.

Then Cody and Alexis—Megan was unfortunate, but it couldn't be helped. And then Grammy, of course. But she was so old, we can't really say if the heart pills would have saved her, even if I had given them to her.

For all her pompous attitude, Adrienne went down easy. Not as easy as Grammy, of course, but my goodness, even *Whitney* put up more of a struggle—that girl fought like a banshee.

I buried Adrienne's body just off a deserted dirt road, about a two-hour drive away from here—somewhere nobody will ever find her. I was smarter than her about that. I wouldn't put a dead body *in my own home*, for God's sake. Right below the floorboards. How stupid could you possibly be? You don't need to be an MD or PhD to know not to put yourself in danger that way.

After she was gone, I knew I had to find and dispose of Jamison's body. Except I still didn't know where she stashed him. I meant to search her house right after I took care of her. I even kept her keys. But there was no time that night because she had her date coming, and by the next morning, her house was crawling with cops.

I thought for sure the police would find Jamison's dead body. But they never did.

It didn't matter though. The only important thing was that nobody came looking for me. By then, I was already living in Manhattan. The police didn't even question me.

After taking care of the Dr Hale problem, I moved on with my life. I enjoyed life in the big city and my new job. I met Ethan, who knew nothing about my past, and we got married. I was happy.

It was only by chance that I noticed Dr Hale's old house had gone up for sale. I asked Judy about it when I saw the house on her website, and she said she was getting it cleaned up right now, but it would be ready for showings shortly. I got a chill down my spine at the thought of Judy having free rein over that house. Then I thought about the number of people who would go in and out of it before it was sold. I calculated the odds that somebody might run across Jamison's dead body, wherever Dr Hale hid it.

I don't know how long the video recordings are kept in the casinos, but I was convinced there was a way to connect me and Jamison. I wasn't about to risk giving birth to my baby in prison.

That's when I knew what I had to do. I had to search the house and get rid of the body. Before anyone else could find it. So I picked the night of a blizzard to go out there, hoping Judy would have cleared out because of the weather, knowing I'd have a couple of solid days to search the house.

When I found the hidden room, I thought for sure I had hit the jackpot. I hadn't. But I found something even more important. If anyone heard that tape of Dr Hale blackmailing me, I would be finished. They would hold me responsible for her murder and Jamison's. Nobody can ever hear this tape except me.

And now I know where she stashed the body. But unfortunately, I don't think I can move it. It was one thing to throw Adrienne Hale in the trunk of my car just after I killed her, but I don't think I can go anywhere near that rotting corpse. The vomit wasn't an act. It was sickening. And then there's Luke Strauss. The boyfriend, who I didn't know was squatting in this house. I'm the only one who knows for sure he wasn't the one who killed Dr Hale. He probably really did love her.

He knows about the dead body. And he knows it isn't Adrienne Hale's body. Luke is a smart guy.

I have to plan my next move very carefully.

CHAPTER 51

It's been well over an hour, and Ethan still isn't back yet. I'm getting worried. The temperature has dropped precipitously over the last hour, and the snow is turning to ice. What if he slipped and hurt himself? What if he's lying out there in the snow, unable to go for help?

And it would be all my fault. After all, I'm the one who brought us here. And I didn't even do what I meant to accomplish. Jamison's body is still lying underneath the floorboards.

The worst part is that I have no phone service or way to find help. I already knew that the service out here was terrible, and I was counting on that. If Ethan could have made a call, he would have called Judy and found out we never had an appointment for last night. Or he would have called for a plow and I would not have had enough time to look for the body.

Now what seemed like an advantage has come back to bite me. I don't know what has happened to Ethan.

And there's nothing I can do. I feel so helpless. I planned things out so perfectly at that cabin and on the night I killed Adrienne. How did I screw this up so badly? It must be pregnancy brain.

I pace across the kitchen, pushing away waves of nausea. I don't know why they call it morning sickness when it's all the freaking time. What am I going to do about Ethan? What if he never comes back?

I may need Luke to help me in that situation. But I don't trust him. He didn't kill Dr Hale, but the fact that he cared so much about her makes him dangerous. Plus he's smart. If he figures out what I've done …

Just when I'm about to go out of my mind, I hear a knock at the front door. I don't know if it's Ethan or if it's the police telling me there's been a horrible accident, but either way, it's someone. It's better than being trapped here, not knowing what's going on.

I almost faint from relief when I see Ethan standing at the front door, the black beanie still covering his golden hair. I throw my arms around him, and he laughs and hugs me back. But I'm not laughing.

'I was so worried!' I bury my face in his dark jacket, which is slightly damp. 'You were gone for such a long time.'

'I'm sorry, Tricia.' His arms feel warm and comforting surrounding me. 'It took longer than I thought. The snow was hard to walk in.'

'So what happened?'

He pulls his phone out of his pocket. 'I got reception right before hitting the main road. I found the number of a local place that does plowing. They're going to come first thing in the morning.'

'In the morning?' I cry.

'I know.' He sighs. 'But the blizzard hit this town hard. Even the main road was a disaster. It probably wouldn't even be safe to drive until the morning.'

He's right. But I hate the idea of sleeping here with a man tied up downstairs.

'But do you want to hear the strangest thing?' he says.

'What?'

He yanks his hat off his hair, which is messy in the sexiest possible way. Despite everything, I feel a stirring inside me. 'The plowing place was all booked up when I called them. But get this—they already had a reservation for them to come here tomorrow morning.'

'That's strange …'

I'm lying. I was the one who called and booked the plow for Sunday morning. I did it before even leaving on our trip, knowing we would be stuck here. I was certain I would have found the body by then and taken care of it. Unfortunately, that did not work out according to plan.

Ethan crinkles his brow. 'Do you think Judy called for the plow?'

Unlikely, considering Judy doesn't even know we're here. The extra keys Ethan 'discovered' below the plant belonged to Adrienne. 'Probably.'

'In any case, it's already been paid for.' Yes, it has. In cash.

I start to bite on my thumbnail, but I put it away. My mother always said that's a nasty habit. 'Did you call the police?'

He shakes his head, and I let out another quick sigh of relief. 'I figure we can call in the morning.'

Ethan has no idea that his wife is responsible for the dead body in the office.

It looks like we're not getting out of here tonight, but at least we'll be able to go first thing in the morning. Thankfully, I've destroyed the worst of the tapes.

As for the dead body, I'm not sure what to do about it yet. But I have a feeling the solution will come to me. It usually does.

CHAPTER 52

For dinner, we eat another meal of cold cuts, heated briefly in the microwave. It wasn't the best thing I've ever eaten, but we're getting out of here in the morning. Tomorrow night, we'll go someplace really nice. We need to celebrate the family we'll be having soon.

After we finish eating, we're about to head upstairs when we hear shouting coming from Dr Hale's office. It's Luke, still trapped in there, although we haven't checked on him.

'Hey!' his crackly voice calls out. 'Anybody there?'

We exchange looks. Ethan drops a hand onto my back and steers me away from the office.

'Hey!' Luke shouts again. 'I'm thirsty! Can I have some water?'

I stop in my tracks a few feet from the door. 'We could give him some water.'

Ethan's jaw tightens. 'He won't die in there, Tricia. He'll be out in the morning—he can hang on until then.'

'Yeah, but … we could at least bring him a glass of water. Let him have a drink.'

'You're too nice.'

I almost laugh at the irony of his statement. I'm glad he thinks that way about me. 'I just think it would be a good idea to give him a few sips of water. We could hold it up for him. We don't have to untie him.'

'You think that's a good idea?' He jerks a thumb in the direction of the door. 'We don't know what's going on in there. What if he got his arms free and he's waiting to jump us the second we get inside?'

I don't think that's true. First of all, the door isn't locked. If he got free from the duct tape, he could just leave. He doesn't need us to let him out. I think he's still bound up in there.

'Please help me!' Luke calls out. 'Just one sip of water! Please!'

I wring my hands together. This is making me uncomfortable. I may have killed a few people, but I didn't torture them. Well, maybe a little. But all of them deserved it. I'm not sure Luke deserves it.

'And I gotta take a piss!' Luke adds.

Now Ethan laughs at my expression. 'You want to help him with that too?'

I guess not.

Ethan gets close to the door to the office. He brings his lips close to the opening and calls out, 'You're not getting any water. You can piss in your pants.'

That response sets up a string of profanities that makes me glad we decided not to go into the office. The pressure on my back from Ethan's hand increases, and I let him lead me away from the office door, toward the staircase.

'Don't let him manipulate you,' Ethan says. 'He isn't a good person. He killed his girlfriend. He killed one of the people closest to him. What kind of person does that?' Ethan doesn't have a clue that Luke isn't the one who killed Dr Adrienne Hale. And he also doesn't know that the body under the floorboards doesn't belong to Dr Hale. 'He's evil,' Ethan adds for emphasis. 'He doesn't deserve water.'

'Yeah,' I mumble.

'You're too nice,' he says again.

We head up the stairs to the bedroom. Yet another night sleeping in Adrienne Hale's bedroom. Even though she blackmailed me and threatened me, I feel guilty about it. I feel guilty about sleeping in her bed. If anyone is capable of coming back as an angry spirit, it's Dr Hale.

When I get into the master bedroom, I pull off the beautiful white cashmere sweater. I curse under my breath when I notice the little yellow stain on one sleeve from the mustard we used on our sandwiches tonight. I bring the sweater into the bathroom and run the sleeve under hot water, rubbing at it to get it out.

It won't come out. Somehow, the stain has already set in. The pristine white cashmere sweater is ruined.

'Tricia?' Ethan peeks his head into the bathroom. 'What are you doing?'

'There's a stain on this sweater. I'm trying to get it out.'

'Why bother? It's not like she's going to be wearing it again.'

Well, he's right. But I keep scrubbing at the stain, hoping it will come out. After a minute, Ethan comes into the bathroom to join me. He comes up behind me, slipping his arms up around my waist. He drops his head and kisses my neck. Once, twice … then his lips linger there.

'Ethan,' I murmur.

'Come on, Tricia. We both need something to take our minds off of everything that just happened.'

Well.

That's true.

CHAPTER 53

I wake up at two in the morning, and I'm alone in the bedroom.

For a second, I am completely disoriented. I had forgotten where I was. I forgot that I'm in Adrienne Hale's house and not my own. That I came here to get rid of Edward Jamison's body, and not only have I failed to do that, but we have also acquired a man tied up in her office.

What a mess. I seriously need help.

I squint around the bedroom, my eyes adjusting to the dark. Ethan isn't in the bed, and I don't see him anywhere else in the room. He's not in the bathroom either. Where did he go?

Maybe he couldn't sleep. Maybe he got up during the night and decided to do some work on his laptop. It makes sense.

Except I don't think that's where he is.

I grab Dr Hale's red robe and wrap it around myself. Then I slide my feet into her fuzzy slippers. It's amazing how easy it's suddenly become to use her stuff. Good thing her clothes are the same size as mine, although she was thinner than me. The woman was practically a skeleton, but she had a certain austere beauty.

When I get out into the hallway, it's dark, but my eyes have adjusted so I leave the lights off. I hear movement coming from downstairs, but it doesn't sound like anything bad is going on. It doesn't sound like Luke has gotten himself free and has attacked my husband.

I descend the stairwell as quietly as I can. When I get to the bottom, Ethan is crouched down in front of the fireplace. All alone. He's fiddling with something, and it takes me a moment to realize he's trying to light a match. The portrait of Adrienne Hale is still propped up against the wall next to the fireplace, her green eyes facing the wall. The portrait was my mother's idea. I thought it was completely ridiculous—who would want a gigantic portrait of themselves? But Dr Hale loved it. She put it right over her mantel immediately. Of course she did. She was that full of herself.

I hope I never have to look at it again.

There's a flash of fire, and then a moment later, the entire fireplace lights up. Ethan stands up and brushes off his hands on his jeans. By his posture, I can tell he's satisfied with the job he did. I wonder how long he's been trying to get the fire going.

I stand there in the shadows, not letting on that I'm watching him. But I see everything. I see him pick up an object from the coffee table and toss it into the fire. Then another. And another.

When he's done, he stands in front of the fireplace, watching. Making sure it burns.

'Ethan,' I say.

He steps away from the fireplace, blinking furiously. His mouth falls open at the sight of me. 'Tricia,' he manages.

I round the side of the couch to come closer to him. 'What are you doing?'

'I ...'

He casts an anxious look at the fireplace. The objects he tossed into the fire haven't yet finished burning, so I can see what they are. But I don't need to look. I already know what he burned in the fire.

It's cassette tapes. Several dozen of them. All emblazoned with the initials GW.

GW was a patient of Dr Hale's for several years. She nursed paranoid delusions that somebody was trying to kill her, including her own son.

GW. Gail Wiley. Ethan's mother.

'I just ...' Beads of sweat break out on Ethan's forehead as he tries to come up with a lie. 'I just think some of those tapes ...'

He doesn't know that I know. That I've always known. I ran into Gail a few times at the house when I was leaving an appointment and she was arriving for hers. Not only was she paranoid but she had a big mouth. She told me all about her concerns that several people in her life were out to end her life, including her son, Ethan. *Dr Hale says I'm paranoid, but he's got money problems—he could use the big insurance payout. And he hates me. I know he does.*

I laughed it off, especially when I caught a glimpse of the handsome Ethan dropping Gail off for one of her appointments. Nobody who looked like *that* could be a bad person. And how nice of him to drop his mother off for her therapy sessions. Of course, he didn't know what she was talking about to the therapist, and he *certainly* didn't know that the sessions were being recorded.

But then a couple of months after Dr Hale's disappearance, my mother, who ran in the same social circles as Gail, told me the gossip about her untimely death. She took a spill down a flight of stairs and broke her neck after she had a few too many drinks. Leaving her son, Ethan, with a hefty insurance payout to take care of the consequences of his first failed startup and then some.

I have to admit, I became a little obsessed with Ethan after that. First of all, he was gorgeous. And second, something about him reminded me of myself. He went after what he wanted. Even if he had to do something other people would say was unthinkable.

Okay, I was more than a little obsessed with Ethan. Let's just say that our coincidental meeting wasn't such a coincidence. More like it was carefully engineered by yours truly.

But he never quite came around the way I wanted him to. After we got married, I thought he would confess everything to me. I thought he would love and trust me enough to tell me the truth. But he hasn't.

That's why I brought him along on this trip. I could have gone alone, and it would've been easier. I could have searched to my heart's content. But I wanted Ethan here with me. He forgot about this house until he saw the portrait of Dr Hale on the wall. But now he knows that his secret is out there.

'What are you doing?' I ask him again. He opens his mouth, but before any words can come out, I add, 'Don't lie.'

'I would never lie to you, Tricia,' he sputters. I give him a look.

His shoulders sag. 'You listened to my mother's tapes, didn't you?'

'Yes. Some of them.'

'Oh God.' He tugs at the short strands of his golden hair. 'I know what she said on those tapes. But I didn't—'

'*Don't lie*.'

He stands there for a moment. The only sounds in the room are the fire crackling and his inhale and exhale.

'Fine,' he says. 'I killed her.'

CHAPTER 54

Now that the truth has left his lips, he seems calmer. He's not sweating any more. He's my confident husband again.

You don't know what she was like.' The bitterness seeps through his voice. 'She was insane. My father died when I was a kid, and he got off easy as far as I'm concerned. She was always extremely anxious, always accusing people around her of being out to get her. Including me.' He pauses to look disdainfully at the fire. 'She was an alcoholic too. When she drank, she always thought I was stealing her stuff, and she'd corner me and accuse me. She would tell me I was rotten. A rotten kid who would never amount to anything.'

'I'm sorry,' I murmur.

'To be fair, I *was* stealing her stuff some of the time. I figured if she was going to accuse me either way, I may as well do it.'

This is the other side of my husband. The one he never lets me see. A little thrill goes through me. 'So what happened?'

'I needed money.' He looks down at his hands. 'She never gave me any money. Never gave me *anything* because she didn't trust anyone besides herself. But she had that insurance policy. And you know what? I wouldn't have even done it, except she was so drunk that night. She was yelling at me about what a terrible son I was, and I couldn't help myself. I pushed her down the stairs.'

He lifts his eyes slowly. 'I had parked around the back. I got the hell out of there and didn't call the police until a day later. I told them I couldn't reach her and I was worried. She was long gone by then.'

Now that he's told me the whole story, he drops onto the couch and buries his face in his hands. I sit down beside him and lower my hand onto his back. His shoulders are trembling.

'You hate me now,' he murmurs. 'I can't blame you.'

'No,' I say.

He lifts his face from his hands. His eyes are damp. 'I love you so much, Tricia. I didn't know I was capable of it. I spent my entire childhood hating that woman, and I didn't know I had it in me to love another person. Then I met you, and it was like you're my soulmate.'

'Then why didn't you tell me the truth?'

'I couldn't tell you! You would have left me if you found out.'

'That's not true.' I reach out and take his hand in mine. 'The truth is …'

'Tricia?'

'I already knew.'

His face fills with confusion. This is the moment to tell him everything. I've been scared to, but I don't have a choice. If there was ever a time to tell him, it is now.

So I start at the beginning. About Cody and Alexis. How I became Dr Hale's patient. How she blackmailed me and forced me to do her bidding. The identity of the body under the floorboards. Finally, the true fate of Dr Adrienne Hale and my goal in coming here this weekend. Ethan listens to the entire story, his face an emotionless mask. At some point, he pulls his hand away from mine and puts it in his lap. He doesn't interrupt me once. He lets me tell him everything, and there's a moment when I'm afraid I've gone too far. He killed his mother, yes. But I killed six people and was responsible for the death of one other. One might argue that my sins outweigh his—if they were keeping track.

When I finish talking, Ethan just sits there for a while, staring at the fireplace. I let him mull over what I just told him. He deserves a few minutes to think it over. I quietly cross my fingers and my toes. He will understand. I know he will.

Won't he?

'Wow,' he finally says. He's still staring at the fire.

What is he thinking? Is he going to turn me in to the police? I took a massive chance here tonight. But I thought he loved me too much. And now his child is growing inside me. He would never do that to me.

He wouldn't. I'm almost sure of it. But I'm not certain.

'So what do you think?' I ask.

'I ...' His eyes reflect the flames from the fire. 'I think ...'

I misjudged him. I've made a terrible mistake.

I thought he would understand, but I was wrong. He doesn't understand. Nobody can.

'Ethan?' I whisper.

He rips his blue eyes away from the fire and looks straight into mine. 'I think that guy Luke is going to be a big problem. He knows way too much.'

My heart flutters. 'Yes. *Yes.* I was thinking the same thing.'

'And also …' He is the one who reaches for my hand this time. 'I'm glad I'm here to help you. We can take care of this problem the right way. Together.'

I squeeze his big, warm hand. 'I knew you would know exactly what to do.'

We stand up simultaneously. Ethan walks over to the bookcase, and he picks up the carving knife he left there. He grips the handle with his right hand. His face glows eerily in the crackling light of the fire. I've always wanted a fireplace, but it's not the sort of thing you could have in Manhattan. And this is a beautiful fireplace.

'You know,' I say thoughtfully, 'this house is kind of growing on me. Maybe I could see myself living here after all.'

'Yeah?' His face lights up. 'I was hoping you would say that. Because I feel the same way.' He raises his eyebrows. 'You coming, Tricia?'

'Yes. Just a moment.'

I find my wool coat draped on the edge of the couch. I rifle around in the pockets, and my fingers make contact with the cassette tape I stashed there. I pull it out, looking at my initials on the side of the tape.

I'm a different person now than the girl on the tape. But in other ways, I haven't changed at all.

I close my fingers around the cassette. I walk over to the fireplace, my cheeks absorbing the heat radiating out of the small space. I toss the tape in with the others, onto the slowly disintegrating pile. For a moment, I stand there and watch it burn.

Then I join my husband.

EPILOGUE

TRICIA

TWO YEARS LATER

My daughter, Delilah, loves the garden behind our house. She turned one a few months ago, and she's in this adorable chubby toddler phase where she walks around with her arms out at her sides, about to topple at any moment. I watch her from the rocking chair in front of the house as she does just that—falls to her knees in the soft grass, then gets right back up without missing a beat.

She is a girl with a mission. Right now, her mission is to bring me a daisy she found growing in the grass. She makes it the rest of the way over to me and places one of her tiny hands on my knee.

'Mama,' she says. 'Dis.'

'Yes.' I accept the slightly crumpled daisy. 'It's a flower, darling.'

'Flar,' she repeats. 'That's right.'

She beams up at me. I might be slightly biased, but I think she's the most beautiful child who has ever lived.

She looks a lot like her father. Ethan and I both have blonde hair, but mine comes out of a bottle and his is real. She has his blonde curls—although his hair is cut too short to curl—and his clear blue eyes. She's a spitting image of the way he looked in the baby pictures he finally showed me soon after we bought this house.

She takes such joy in the little things too. I bought her a baby doll for her first birthday, and her little face lit up with a brilliant smile. It made me remember the collection of dolls I used to have as a child. I had at least a dozen of them. And then another collection in a drawer in my room of the shorn heads of the dolls I didn't like as much. 'Flar!' Delilah cries, then she toddles back into the garden, eager to rip out more of my flowers and deliver them to me.

I reach for the iced tea on the glass table by the rocking chair. We kept some of the furniture Adrienne Hale left behind in the house. We kept the bed but got a new mattress. We kept her sectional sofa after sponging it down aggressively. We kept the antique coffee table. I took down the portrait and stashed it in the attic. I couldn't quite bring myself to destroy it.

Unfortunately, Dr Hale didn't have any patio furniture. All that had to be purchased new. But we got a few gorgeous items. Everybody who comes to our house remarks enviously about how beautiful the place is.

They have no idea what a steal it was.

A hand drops onto my shoulder—Ethan is standing next to me. I smile up at him, and his eyes crinkle as he smiles back. He's one of those men who's going to get much more handsome as he gets older. You can just tell.

'Is she being good?'

'She's always good,' I say.

It's true. We live a charmed life here. We have an angelic little daughter. Ethan can work from home most days and avoid a commute into the city. All we had to do to get here was knock off a few people.

Right after our weekend at the house, I called Judy and told her we were very interested in the estate going up for sale. I pressured her to show it to us before it was officially ready for a viewing, and we put in an offer on the spot. We didn't haggle. We paid the asking price, not a penny less.

After all, we had a reason not to want people tromping in and out of the house. We had a reason to keep Judy from discovering any of the hidden compartments and turning the house back into a crime scene. We especially had a reason to keep her out of the garden.

And now it's ours. Our dream house. I don't know how I could've ever not wanted to live here.

'How is the bean doing?' Ethan asks me.

I instinctively lay my right hand on my stomach. A few weeks ago, I found out that Delilah will have a baby brother or sister. We're both ecstatic about it. After all, as Ethan points out, we have four more bedrooms to fill. Dr Hale wasted this house, living here all alone. We will put it to good use.

'The bean is good,' I tell him. He grins at me. 'Glad to hear it.'

Delilah has found another flower to bring to me. But in her eagerness, she takes a worse spill this time and doesn't recover quite as easily. She sits on the grass, her chubby legs stuck out in front of her, wailing until her face turns bright red.

'Oh no!' I cry, my maternal instinct kicking into overdrive. 'Let me grab her.'

'No.' Ethan squeezes my shoulder. 'You rest, Mama. I'll get her.'

I smile and take another sip of my iced tea while my husband sprints into the garden to comfort our daughter. He's *so* good with her. He's sweet and patient, and he makes her laugh. Although, to be fair, it isn't hard to make a one-year-old laugh. Dropping a Cheerio on the floor will do the trick.

Sure enough, after a minute, Ethan has Delilah happy and laughing again. He lifts her onto his shoulders and gives her a ride around the garden while she giggles with delight.

I watch as Ethan's loafers trample over the patch of grass that just started growing back about eight months ago. For a year, we watched that patch anxiously. The grass on the rest of the garden was so lush and green, but nothing grew there.

I looked it up. I told Ethan that after a dead body is buried in the ground, plant growth is suppressed for about a year, but then it comes back even better than before. And it's not like somebody was going to look at that patch of soil where nothing could grow and know that Luke Strauss's body was buried underneath.

Digging his grave was harder than killing him. Ethan took care of both counts—I'd never found him sexier. Luke fought, but not as hard as I would have expected. I saw the resigned look in his eyes seconds before Ethan slashed his throat. And now that he's gone, he's reunited with his precious Adrienne, if you believe in such things. Thankfully, two years later, the grass has grown back where we buried him. His body will act as fertilizer for years to come. As will the body of Edward Jamison, buried a few feet away.

Ethan waves to me from the garden. I love him so much. I never thought it would be possible to love again after what Cody did to me. But here I am. Married to a wonderful man. And the two of us share a secret that will bind us together for the rest of our lives. Both of us will take that secret to our graves.

At least I will.

Sometimes I wonder about Ethan. He gets nervous when people go out into our garden. He was so anxious about the grass, I almost thought he was going to crack for a while. If somebody came around and started asking questions, I'm not sure how he would hold up.

Hopefully, that won't ever happen. But if it does, I'm prepared to take care of the situation.

After all, my mother always said that the only way two people can keep a secret is if one of them is dead

ACKNOWLEDGMENTS

As I was finishing this final draft, I was searching through some of my previous manuscripts for general acknowledgments that I could just kind of copy, because—let's face it—I always thank the same people. Unfortunately, I couldn't find any generic ones. I had one where I was talking about my husband trying to convince me to write about conjoined cow twins, one where I said my father was a serial killer (or wasn't—not clear), and one where I confessed to multiple unsolved murders as well as the locations where I buried the bodies.

(Oh wait, I think I deleted that last one. Never mind.)

Do other authors obsess so much about the acknowledgments? No? Just me? And the weird part is the thanking section only ever ends up being, like, a paragraph.

On that note …

Thank you to my mother for reading and rereading this one. Thanks to Jen for the thorough critique as always, and in general, thanks to my entire Kickass

Women Writers' Power Group (I just made up that name right now, but I think they'll be cool with it), including Beth and Maura. Thanks to Kate for the great suggestions. Thank you to Nelle for a thoughtful critique. Thank you to Avery for critique and cover advice. Thanks to Pam for cover advice and also for your awesome mentorship. Thanks to Val for your eagle eye.

And thank you to my father, who for the first time *ever* read a book I wrote prior to publication so that he could give me advice from the perspective of a practicing psychiatrist, including 'Manolos are *not* boots!' (Yes, they can be. Stick to psychiatry, Dad.)